FOUNDATIONS
OF
CHILD ADVOCACY

FOUNDATIONS
OF
CHILD ADVOCACY

Legal Representation
of the Maltreated Child

Edited by
Donald C. Bross and Laura Freeman Michaels
The National Association of Counsel for Children

Published by Bookmakers Guild, Inc.   Longmont, Colorado

Copyright © 1987, Bookmakers Guild, Inc.

Library of Congress Card Catalog Number 86-070005
ISBN 0-917665-10-4

Published in 1987 in the United States of America by
Bookmakers Guild, Inc.
1430 Florida Avenue, Suite 202
Longmont, Colorado 80501

Printed and bound in the United States of America

CONTENTS

——————— PART I ———————
Knowledge About Childhood

─────── PART II ───────
Issues for the Child Representative

─────── PART III ───────
Standard Procedures for the Child Advocate

ACKNOWLEDGMENTS

The following articles are reprinted in slightly different form from their original publication. We thank the authors and their publishers for allowing us to include them in their present form here.

Bross, D. C.: "Professional and Agency Liability for Negligence in Child Protection" is reprinted with permission from *Law, Medicine & Health Care*, vol. 11, no. 2; © 1983, American Society of Law & Medicine, Boston, MA.

Haralambie, A. M.: "Experts in Custody Cases" is reprinted from *Handling Child Custody Cases*, by Ann M. Haralambie, © 1983 by McGraw-Hill, Inc., by permission of Shepard's McGraw-Hill, Colorado Springs, CO. Further reproduction of any kind is strictly prohibited.

Lane, C. H.: "The Guardian ad Litem in Divorce Cases" is reprinted with portions revised to lend a broader application from the *Advanced Family Law Course Book*, August, 1980, © 1980, State Bar of Texas.

CONTRIBUTORS

Donald C. Bross, J. D., Ph.D.
Mr. Bross is legal counsel to the C. Henry Kempe National Center for the Prevention and Treatment of Child Abuse and Neglect; Associate Professor in Pediatrics (Family Law), School of Medicine, University of Colorado; and Executive Director of the National Association of Counsel for Children.

Laura Freeman Michaels, Esq.
Ms. Michaels is a guardian *ad litem* in Colorado and the Associate Director of the National Association of Counsel for Children.

Edward Goldson, M.D.
Dr. Goldson is a staff pediatrician and member of the child advocacy team at The Children's Hospital in Denver, Colorado.

Ann M. Haralambie, Esq.
Ms. Haralambie is in private practice in Tucson, Arizona. She founded the Arizona Council of Attorneys for Children and is currently president of the National Association of Counsel for Children.

David L. Kerns, M.D.
> Dr. Kerns is the Chairman of the Department of Pediatrics at Santa Clara Valley Medical Center in California. He formerly was the Associate Director of the C. Henry Kempe National Center for the Prevention and Treatment of Child Abuse and Neglect.

Carol Higley Lane, Esq.
> Ms. Lane is a judge for the city of Houston and associate referee for Juvenile Court. She is Chairman-elect of the Juvenile section of the Houston Bar and was President of the National Association of Counsel for Children in 1981-82.

John L. Lawritson, Esq.
> Mr. Lawritson is in private practice in Denver and was formerly a Denver juvenile court judge. He is a former president of the National Association of Counsel for Children and currently serves on the organization's Board of Directors.

Judith C. White, M.A.
> Ms. White is a child protection caseworker for Denver County Department of Social Services.

PREFACE

It is nearly 300 years since publication of what may be the first English book on law relating to children (*The Infants Lawyer; or Law, both Ancient and Modern Relating to Infants,* 1697). For nearly all of the intervening period the few subsequent books that appeared on the subject focused on legal doctrines that had developed concerning, not so much children themselves, as children's property and the rights of adults to some interest in the property or to the custody or guardianship of children. As courts and legislatures produced more law relating to children, especially regarding juvenile crime and child abuse, the legal literature at first failed to reflect the law's increased attention to childhood. Since the tradition of this literature was to expound doctrine, the paucity of legal rules in these new laws provided little of substance to be analyzed, debated or published. Delinquency law that arose during the nineteenth century, first concerned with juvenile corrections and later with juvenile courts, emphasized official discretion rather than rules of law in looking after the welfare of young offenders. Action was to be individualized rather than responsive to the demands of doctrine.

The law of child abuse and neglect, with which this volume is engaged, has similar roots. The rescue of maltreated children was not to follow mechanically from any legislative constella-

tion of rules, but was rather an enterprise entrusted to the
sound judgment of those with child protection responsibilities.
Like delinquency law, the centrality of discretion in child
protection law produced but little legal dogma and, consequently, a dearth of legal literature. Unlike delinquency law,
which is currently experiencing a rapid growth of rules to
replace discretion, however, child protection law remains
largely driven and structured by the discretion of judges and
workers. Definitions of child abuse and neglect, for example,
continue as elusive concepts unrefined by a jurisprudence such
as that which has developed about the definitions of criminal
offenses.

While there has been much speculation over why lawyers
have been drawn into this child protection process, it is clear
that the demands placed on their professional skills extend well
beyond incisive analysis of doctrine which is itself so largely
undeveloped. Especially as advocates for children, members of
the bar find themselves in a position to influence the judgments of other participants in the process, parents and social
workers, as much as judges. To meet this responsibility Dr.
Bross and Ms. Freeman have put together a book that
responds to the question, what do lawyers need to know when
there isn't a great deal of law to know? The essays in this
volume provide the kind of guidance, insight and extra-legal
knowledge that is highly valuable for anyone involved in child
protection, lawyer and non-lawyer alike. As a needed addition
to the legal literature, it is much welcomed.

Sanford J. Fox
Newton, MA
June 1986

INTRODUCTION

Since its inception, the goal of the National Association of Counsel for Children (NACC) has been to establish a better foundation for the independent representation of children involved in court proceedings. The activities of training, publishing, proposing standards and accepting friend-of-the-court positions in special cases contribute to the objective of establishing a strong base of national and international member practitioners who work with the children affected by legal proceedings. The NACC encourages child advocates from varied backgrounds to study issues, compare methods, share resources and referrals, and support children in need of protection.

Foundations of Child Advocacy incorporates themes and practice recommendations which have been accumulated at NACC conferences and in publications since 1977. Some of the materials appear essentially in their original forms with some modifications and updates by the editors. Other chapters were written specifically for this book.

Because of the various complications and issues arising when children become entangled in legal proceedings, many of the authors have focused on the cases in which a determination has been made that the child is not safe to remain in the home. The examination of this stage of the case, however, is done with the understanding that the Adoption Assistance and Child Welfare Act of 1980 (P.A. 96-272) and many state statutes require that state agencies make reasonable efforts to prevent removing a child from the home.

To assist the child representative, Part I offers a working knowledge about the basic business of childhood, health and pathology in children. Insights are provided by professionals from the perspectives of their varied disciplines. Ed Goldson helps us understand the basic parameters of child development as these relate to abuse and neglect. He reminds us of the importance of the social, emotional and psychological impact of child maltreatment, as well as the physical traumas. David Kerns discusses the pediatrician's role, helping us understand what might be expected of physicians, and the range of harms which might be diagnosed. Judith White offers us the social worker's perspective, explaining the special relationship that the worker must maintain to assist and treat children and their families. Definitions of abuse and neglect from a legal perspective are analyzed by Donald Bross.

Part II of *Foundations of Child Advocacy* covers some of the basic legal aspects of child representation. Following Donald Bross's chapter on the importance of child advocacy in court, Laura Freeman Michaels discusses the evidentiary issues likely to be encountered by the child's representative. In turn, Donald Bross examines the different ways a case is handled when the child is a court witness or when the decision is made not to have the child testify. Underlining the importance of expert testimony, Ann Haralambie gives many practical hints on working with expert witnesses. In her chapter on child representation in divorce custody cases, Carol Higley Lane recognizes that children in need of protection can enter the courts through different avenues, and some aspects of child representation can be generalized for varied legal settings. In addition, Donald Bross points out liability considerations for those serving children and emphasizes the need for accountability in the child's representation.

Practical advocacy aids, standardized guidelines and forms are included in Part III.

In the past, members of the National Association of Counsel for Children and speakers at NACC conferences have made many fine contributions to furthering the rights of children and the role of the child's representative. To those un-named advocates who have lent their time, suggestions and support, we are indeed grateful. We regret that all of these could not appear in this single volume. Nevertheless, *Foundations of Child Advocacy* must stand for the many who have contributed their time, energy, and caring to the representation of children.

Donald C. Bross
Laura Freeman Michaels

PART I

Knowledge About Childhood

CHILD DEVELOPMENT AND THE RESPONSE TO MALTREATMENT

Edward Goldson, M.D.

During the last fifteen years the legal profession has paid increasing attention to child abuse. There has also been an increased concern by child-care providers and advocates as to the possible effects that abuse itself and the legal process may have on the child. The most pressing question that must be addressed is how those in the legal profession can best meet the needs of the abused child. In order to meet those needs, some understanding of normal child development is necessary.

BASIC ASSUMPTIONS

There are numerous schools of thought dealing with child development. It is not the purpose of this discussion to elaborate all of these theories. Instead, some of the developmental processes children undergo and the issues children must address are briefly reviewed. In addition, the implications these aspects of childhood may have for lawyers representing maltreated children are noted.

It has long been recognized that all children follow general patterns of motor, cognitive and emotional development.

There are basic "developmental milestones" that usually need to be achieved in order for the next task level to be attempted and ultimately mastered. Although development occurs in a seemingly linear pattern with the child progressing from relatively simple to more complex behaviors, the "nitty gritty" of development takes place in spurts and plateaus. A child may master a particular developmental task and then plateau at that level before making another developmental leap. Indeed, some children may develop rapidly, plateau, even seem to regress, and then have another rapid period of development. Although all development leads to more complex functioning, not all areas of development will necessarily proceed at the same rate. Thus, a child may make rapid strides in the achievement of new skills in one area of development, for example, in gross motor function, while not seeming to make much progress in a different area, such as language.

Although development is predictable to some extent, it remains multidimensional and complex. As a result, it is almost impossible to encompass and address all of its parameters at the same time. Thus, development has been divided into its various component parts that can then be more easily monitored. The usual parameters of development that have been monitored, at least in the young child, include the individual's gross and fine motor skills, his adaptive or problem-solving capabilities, his speech/language development and his personal/social functioning. At what age does a child walk? When does a child talk in sentences? When does a child achieve object permanence, that is, understand that an object or person exists although they may not be in the child's presence? Norms have been established for the acquisition of these skills so that one can determine whether or not an individual child is, or is not, achieving developmental milestones as compared to his peers. For those concerned with the impact of various stresses on the child, it becomes important to be familiar with these milestones and to know at what ages they are usually achieved. Numerous resources that provide this information are available. Some of these are listed in the bibliography.

THEORIES AND APPROACHES
TO CHILD DEVELOPMENT

Piaget

Just as there are clinically defined developmental milestones for the parameters noted above, so there are conceptual and clinical milestones or stages for cognitive and psychosocial development. One of the most influential theoreticians in the area of child development was Jean Piaget,[1] the Swiss psychologist, philosopher and epistemologist. Through observations of his own children as well as other normal children, Piaget constructed a model of cognitive development that is independent of psychosocial and socioeconomic factors. With this model he attempted to encompass the areas of childhood cognition: language, abstract thinking, mathematics, moral development, etc.

Piaget's thinking is strongly grounded in biological concepts in the sense that he transferred two features of biological evolution to his theories of child development. First, he noted that old structures fit into new functions under changed circumstances. Development is rooted in what already exists and is continuous with the past. At the same time, structures change to fit new demands. Second, Piaget determined that adaptations do not occur in isolation. Rather, they evolve in response to environmental demands.

In nature there are biological structures that evolve to meet new demands. The behavioral parallel that Piaget draws he defines as the *schema*. Schema can be reliable behavioral responses to given stimuli, such as the sucking reflex. However, schema are usually more complicated and generally include a variety of acts in many different circumstances, not just the response to a specific stimulus. Moreover, schema are *mobile*. That is, particular schema can be applied to a variety of objects of stimuli, even some not previously encountered. Moreover, the mobility of a schema increases when it is used for obtaining some goal. Thus, the child's behavior becomes more complex and also more adaptable as he attempts more complex behaviors. The simplest schema, in some sense, are the *sensorimotor* schema. They involve overt actions in terms of manipulating the environment. However, there are also cognitive schema, such as the concepts of space, numbers, morality, or the laws of logic. In a word, the schema is a complex concept encompassing both overt motor behaviors and internalized thought processes. When these internal actions become integrated into a logical system, they are considered to be logical operations. The child who is able to use such a system of operations is said to be in the stage of concrete or formal operations.

The schema represents the structure that adapts. Assimilation and accommodation are the processes of adaptation. Assimilation describes the child's capability to handle new situations and new tasks and problems using her existing skills and means of coping. Accommodation describes the process by which the child is able to manage those situations that are too difficult. Assimilation means that the child has already adapted and can handle the situation with which she is presented. Accommodation, on the other hand, means that the child has to change in order to adapt. What is important to bear in mind is that the two processes are interrelated in that the child must be able to assimilate a new situation before she can accommodate to it and so adapt.

One of the questions that arises is why does a child attempt to perform a particular motor or psychological task? Generally, the child becomes stimulated or motivated by a novel, yet assimilable, task which activates a schema. The child then works at mastering the task, such as grasping a pellet. However, once this is easily accomplished, it is no longer motivating and the child then moves on to other tasks that attract her and motivate her to expand her schema, and so enable her to perform increasingly complex tasks. In summary then, according to Piaget, the child has evolving cognitive structures called schema that adapt to new situations in the environment. The manner in which this adaptation occurs involves two interrelated processes, assimilation and accommodation.

Piaget describes four distinct stages in the development of cognitive functioning that are associated with relatively distinct periods in the child's life. The first stage is the sensorimotor period, which extends, more or less, from birth to two years. During this period the child acquires skills and adaptations of an overt behavioral nature based on the organization of sensory and motor information. The infant becomes able to coordinate information from the various sensory modalities and integrate the motor behavior of different parts of the body. So, for example, the infant becomes able to look at what he is listening to, or is able to hold his hand still so that he can then look at the object being held and can integrate the two hands to work cooperatively. Another acquisition that the child makes during this period is the recognition of the world as a permanent, stable place—not one whose existence is dependent upon his perceiving it. Thus, the infant recognizes that if an object is covered, it still exists even though he cannot see it, or that mother still exists even if she is not in his presence. Finally, the child develops the capacity to engage in goal-directed behavior that is governed by some intention. During this period the infant evolves from an organism that is very much dependent on biologically determined reflexes to one who is able to organize and manipulate a world that has distinct boundaries. Although the child makes great strides in his capacity to know, he does not yet have a truly cognitive or conceptual representation of the world. The world for him is concrete, and the child relates to it in a practical "hands-on" manner which is action-oriented.

The second stage is the preoperational period, which extends approximately from two to seven years, during which the child's internal cognitive picture of the external world gradually grows until the various discrete concepts become organized into interrelated systems. The child learns to think of more than one idea at a time and also begins to master representations rather than dealing only with concrete objects. Although the child is now developing language, he is not yet able to engage in logical thinking. Rather the child is egocentric, important and powerful, and tends to view the world anthropomorphically. Goblins and ghosts are real and alive. Everything in the world is alive and has its own volition. Indeed, the child has to learn the word "dead" since everything to him is alive. But the child does not yet understand the irreversibility of death or even other losses. Morally, the child does things or understands the "do's and don'ts" simply because the authority figure says this is so. The child is punishment and obedience oriented. You must not break the rules or else you will be punished. There is no real awareness of other people's interests and no recognition that others' views might differ from one's own.

The next advance in the development of the child's cognitive structures is when she enters the stage of concrete operations, which lasts from about age seven to eleven years. During this period formal thought processes emerge such that the child becomes logical. She learns how to order objects by size and shape. She understands some of the simple relationships between classes of objects. She acquires a rudimentary concept of time and space, which will be fundamental to her understanding of how objects and events are ordered. However, the child during this period does not yet have the capacity to grasp such concepts as volume, which involves an understanding of quantity and density, nor can she utilize the scientific method, which involves holding certain variables constant while others are manipulated. Morally, she begins to understand and internalize the differences between right and wrong without being totally influenced by peers and adults.

In my observation abused delinquents are much forced into this sooner than the avg. person

The final stage into which most children (but not all) pass is that of formal operations, the most abstract level of thinking. Children enter this stage at approximately 11 years of age and go on to achieve the capacity for causal and abstract thinking. They can perform experiments and deduce the proper implications of their endeavors. In essence, the child finally has a fundamental grasp of logical thought that then will expand as the child grows and matures.

The above brief discussion highlights the fact, if one accepts Piaget's scheme, that at different ages children have varying cognitive capacities and that developmental changes emerge from the interaction between cognitive structures, or schema, and the child's environment. What also becomes important to bear in mind is the process that facilitates the child's development. That is, there is an ongoing interaction between an active, motivated child and his surroundings. To the extent that the child can act upon/assimilate his environment, he can develop his cognitive capacities. The process of development entails the child's emerging map of the world and of the construction of his own intelligence. In order to achieve this task the child has to establish a partnership with his environment and his caretakers, namely his parents. In order for the child to succeed, that environment has to first recognize and allow the child to be an active agent in the construction of his intelligence, of his self and of his world map. Second, the environment must be such that it fits and stretches the child's cognitive capacities. The child must work, but he also must be able to succeed. If the world is unreliable, confusing, provides mixed messages or is unsafe, physically and emotionally, then the normal processes described by Piaget are inhibited and the growth of the child's cognitive capacities are constrained. When this occurs the child is placed at a disadvantage developmentally, which influences not only his cognitive development and ultimate functioning, but also his emotional development.

Thus, in recognizing the process and the stages through which children pass, the legal professional may have to tailor his expectations to the child's level of functioning. One cannot expect a child of two to make moral judgments and be able to understand the abstract concepts which a nine-year-old child might understand. On the other hand, a four-year-old may have the cognitive capacity to describe his experiences and to have some understanding as to what has taken place.

Bowlby and Ainsworth

Another theory of the child's development that has come to the fore in recent years has been the role of attachment as put forth by Bowlby and Ainsworth.[2] These authors have postulated that in order for the infant to be able to relate to and feel secure in her environment, the child must, and indeed does, become attached to her caretakers. This attachment is reflected in such behaviors as demonstrating a marked preference for the particular caretaker, by being upset when that individual is not available, by feeling secure in her interactions with the outside world when the caretaker is present, and being able to more readily explore and interact with the world once a secure attachment has been established with significant, nurturing others. Moreover, there is a significant body of literature that has demonstrated, at least in the preschool years, that the development of attachment does exist and that it influences later behavior. A number of authors using various real-life situations and experimental models have shown that if normal attachment does not take place, the child is at risk for the development of various psychopathologies.

The theory of attachment is based on an ethological model which suggests that the infant has certain innate behaviors to which the adult inherently responds. With appropriate, consistent and sensitive responses, the child learns to respond in turn to the adult who then responds to the infant in a contingent, predictable manner, thus establishing a "dialogue" with the infant, which leads to the development of attachment. With the establishment of this relationship to an adult, the child is then enabled to explore and interact with the larger world and expand her horizons. Under normal circumstances, the child is able to expend her energies in mastering her world and, in a sense, developing her map and constructing her intelligence. When these conditions are not present, the child must, instead, spend time gauging her world, looking for consistencies, and always being on the alert for how she can best function in a confusing world; i.e., an abusive environment. This, indeed, deprives the child from securely exploring her world and limits her experiences. Such children are often hyperalert, overly solicitous and frequently engage in role reversal with their adult caretakers.

Erikson

A third theory of child development that addresses personality development is that put forth by Erik Erikson in his essay, "Eight Ages of Man."[3] Erikson makes two assumptions about the development of the individual's personality.

> 1) . . . that the human personality in principle develops according to steps predetermined in the growing person's readiness to be driven toward, to be aware of, and to interact with, a widening social radius; and 2) that society in principle, tends to be so constituted as to meet and invite this succession of potentialities for interaction and attempts to safeguard and to encourage the proper rate and the proper sequence of their enfolding."[4]

Furthermore, Erikson maintains that all of us pass through, or can pass through, eight stages as we traverse our life span. However, these stages continually exist in relation to one another, rather than as permanent achievements. There are certain periods in life when the particular issues come into critical focus for the individual and when he is ready and capable of addressing these issues. Also, those are periods when the resolution of conflict may have long-term consequences. However, all of these issues continue to exist and influence each other throughout life.

During the first age all children must deal with issues of basic trust versus mistrust. In more analytic terms this is the oral sensory period through which infants and toddlers pass. The second age is that of autonomy versus shame and doubt, which corresponds to the muscular-anal period. This period also coincides with preschool when the child's motor skills are becoming more adept and he is beginning to deal with separation and individuation, as well as with the development of autonomy. The third age finds the child in the early school years. This period is identified as the age of initiative versus guilt, and it coincides with the locomotor-genital period. It is a time of experimentation. The world is enlarging and the child is being exposed to many new experiences in which he takes the initiative in motor and mental behavior. The fourth stage, called the age of industry versus inferiority, is associated with "latency" in analytic terms. This period finds the child well into school life. The child becomes a worker. It is a time when systematic instruction takes place, which allows the child to acquire those skills that will ultimately enable him to function in his world. With the advent of puberty the child enters the fifth period called the age of identification versus role confusion. The remaining ages include the age of intimacy versus isolation, the age of generativity versus stagnation, and finally the age of ego integrity versus despair. These coincide with young adulthood, adulthood and maturity.

In reviewing the various views of how children develop, we see that all address some aspect of increasingly complex and abstract function that is based on the evolution of physical structures, cognitive structures and psychological tasks. Erikson, Piaget, the attachment theorists and those who look at general development, all speak to an inherent drive toward complexity that is predetermined, but which, in order to evolve, must interact with the environment. Inherent in all of these arguments is the fact that children, at different ages, have different capacities.

TASKS OF CHILDHOOD

Drawing on what has just been presented, what then are the developmental tasks of the child from birth to six years of age? First, the child must acquire basic motor skills and the foundations of language. The physical world must be perceived as being stable and secure with clearly defined boundaries that the child can understand and master. He must be able to become attached to meaningful caregivers and establish a sense of trust. As the child continues to grow and mature he must acquire increasing motor and adaptive skills on which he can rely. Also he has to acquire, at least, prelogical language and deal with the concepts of life and death and time. This is also a period in the child's life when his thinking is very concrete and when he sees himself as being all powerful and the center of the world. These are normal phenomena, but place the child at risk when his world goes awry. Not infrequently when there is family conflict, disorder and parental strife, the child believes he is at fault. Consequently he assumes the responsibility for the disorder and also the guilt. The child often will attempt to intervene to make things good, an effort which, of course, is doomed to failure. On the other hand, the child may become withdrawn and have many somatic and psychological symptoms resulting from the conflict and from his inability to correct the situation.

If one accepts that these are the essential tasks for the child during this period of life, what then are the environmental and psychological conditions essential for this growth to occur? There are two critical issues for the child: the continuity and stability of relationships and the environment, and the child's concept of time.

It is apparent, both from experience and from the literature, that continuity and predictability of relationships and environmental stability are critical for a child's development. Central to the list of tasks each child has at different ages is the need for consistency and continuity. In order for a child to develop trust, to establish attachment to significant figures in the environment, to be able to explore the environment knowing that it is safe and that there are those who will protect him, a child must have a continuity of relationships. These do not always have to reside in only one person, but certainly must involve a limited number of individuals to whom the infant and young child can turn and be assured of consistent, sensitive and appropriate response to his needs. Furthermore, it has been shown that when this continuity of relationship does not exist, children fail to establish meaningful attachments, tend to be superficial in their relationships, insecure and have limited capacity to explore their environments. The early periods described by Erikson, Piaget and the attachment theorists form the cornerstones for later development. If a child cannot or does not trust, then he cannot develop the strengths to venture afield to explore. If he does not explore, his range of experiences becomes limited and constrained, and so he does not adapt, assimilate, learn, expand his horizons or construct his world map and his own intelligence. In a word, when the child finds himself in an abusive environment he must expend an enormous amount of emotional and physical energy just to cope! This then limits the amount of energy available to explore the environment in all of its many facets.

The child's sense of time and the adult's understanding of that sense become very critical for the child's development and also her capacity to establish meaningful relationships. Most adults have the capacity to anticipate the future and to manage delay. Children, particularly the child under six years of age, do not have this capacity. Rather the child has a built-in urgency to meet her emotional or physical needs immediately. This is certainly consistent with what we know about the child's cognitive structure at these ages. For an infant or toddler, absence from a primary caretaker or attachment figure for more than a few days is more than she can tolerate. The child is dependent on others to meet her needs. When those needs are not met in accordance with her time frame, she becomes stressed. The infant's "memory" does not go beyond that time, and so she is not able to hold onto the parent or caretaker she has lost. Consequently, the infant or toddler who is continually being moved from one caretaker to the other is denied the opportunity to develop and sustain any kind of meaningful relationship. Thus, she experiences multiple losses at a time when it is essential for her psychological growth and development to have a continuity of those relationships.

The older child, from two to five, has a greater capacity to sustain the memory of the attachment figure, but even for this child, an absence for more than two months becomes intolerable and the preexisting relationship is ended with the associated grieving, sense of loss and resultant scarring. The school-age child will be able to tolerate greater periods of absence, but for any child an absence of more than one year is tantamount to complete loss.

> The significance of parental absences depends, then, upon their duration, frequency, and the developmental period during which they occur. The younger the child, the shorter is the interval before a leave-taking will be experienced as a permanent loss accompanied by feelings of helplessness and profound deprivation. Since a child's sense of time is directly related to his capacity to cope with breaches in continuity, it becomes a factor in determining if, when, and with what urgency the law should act.[5]

Two other issues that must be considered in the development of the child are the presence of an intact central nervous system (CNS) and good health. Much of what has been discussed is based on the fact that the child has a normal CNS. When this is present the child then has a normal repertoire of neuro-motor behaviors and also has the capacity for the development of the normal cognitive structures that enable him to interact with the environment and to process motor-sensory stimuli in such a way as to allow for normal development. It also means that the caretaker is able to interact with an infant, and then a child, in a way that is familiar, that has been learned and for which there are existing models, and allows for the establishment of age-appropriate interactions. The corollary then also holds. Namely, that the child with a damaged or compromised CNS does not have the breadth of repertoire, that her responses are different, and even deviant, from the norms and what would be expected. Therefore, the caretaker has a far more difficult task in his interactions with the infant, thus entering the relationship handicapped and stressed.

The second important condition for normal development is good health. Sick children are not at their best! The ill child tends to be less interactive, less consistent in her responses and less willing to engage the environment. The chronically ill child is at risk for malaise and depression, for developmental regression and for not developing to her maximum potential. Furthermore, sick children are stressed children, which also means that their families are going to be stressed. The rearing of children is never an easy task. The rearing and caring for a sick child is even more difficult.

SUMMARY AND DISCUSSION

How then is all of this relevant to the legal profession? The general developmentalists, Piaget, Bowlby and Ainsworth, and Erikson address different aspects of the child's development. Yet there are a number of parallels in their thinking. They all address the child's movement from basic skills and needs to more complex levels of functioning. They address the issues of sensitive or critical periods and the need for stability, security and reciprocity during these periods. For example, during the first stage of psychosocial development, during which the child is dealing with the issue of trust versus mistrust (Erikson), if a child is unable to establish a meaningful attachment to consistent figures (Bowlby and Ainsworth), then one could hypothesize that the child will have difficulty accomplishing the tasks set forth during the sensorimotor period (Piaget). Consequently, the child has a limited capacity to attend to the world, a poor sense of self, will probably be on the defensive vis-á-vis his environment, and thus be inhibited and constrained in his interactions with the world. The lawyer involved in litigation around children and families must understand something about these dynamics. With both an understanding of the critical psychosocial conflicts a child is experiencing and an understanding of the child's cognitive capacities, the lawyer can more effectively advocate for and protect the child when the child's needs and well-being are threatened.

Lawyers, by and large, become involved with families when there is some disorder such that the state has to intervene. Conditions that may necessitate the state's involvement include child abuse in the forms of nonaccidental trauma, neglect, failure-to-thrive or sexual abuse. In other situations a child may have no biological family available for reasons of parental death or abandonment. Consequently, a permanent placement must be found for the child. Under these circumstances, the lawyer with an understanding of normal child development and of the issues and tasks that the child has to accomplish can make a significant contribution to the child's development and ultimate capacity to develop into an independent, well-functioning adult. The legal process can be a long and tedious one. Adults can tolerate such a process; a child cannot. The young child who is in the sensorimotor period of development and is engaged in establishing basic trust and achieving basic motor and cognitive landmarks cannot tolerate, without significant scarring, prolonged separations and intermittent engagements with multiple caretakers with whom he is being temporarily placed. Thus, the lawyer involved in such a case must become the child's advocate and be able to facilitate the legal process so that the child is not damaged or compromised by a system whose goals should be to protect the child, but which sometimes may permit adults to lose sight of the child's needs and capacities. For example, in requiring a child to testify, a lawyer must be able to recognize whether or not a child has the appropriate cognitive skills and capacity to respond to the questions asked of him and to make the necessary moral judgments. On the other hand, the lawyer must not minimize the child's capacities.

In order to make these decisions and to act in the child's best interests, an understanding of development is important. A brief overview has been presented in the preceding pages. However, along with an understanding of the general concepts of child development, the child's attorney or legal advocate needs to engage consultants expert in their understanding of children and families. This is essential for the successful adjudication of cases involving children. Pediatricians, psychologists, psychiatrists and social workers, among others, should be involved in the objective assessment and care of such children and their families. They must be able to support the child, to understand what he is feeling and to see how the events are influencing his behavior and development. It must also be recognized that what the child is experiencing is occurring over time and that the child's time reference is much shorter than that of the adult. Also, as noted above, young children have a sense of self-power, and they often will believe all things happening are their fault or are the result of their behavior. They need to be repeatedly reassured that bad or unpleasant occurrences are not their fault. They need to be cared for in a safe physical and psychological environment— one which is consistent and nurturing rather than variable, changing and unpredictable. Court experiences should be made as untraumatic as possible. Prolonged separation from significant caretakers should be minimized and long, drawn-out legal processes should be curtailed. The child should be interviewed in ways that are age-appropriate and sensitive to his needs and understanding. These are things that a knowledgeable, sensitive child advocate can facilitate and accomplish.

There is no question that there are circumstances in which children will have to be separated from their caretakers— usually parents. What we know from the child development literature and general experience suggests that children's needs, their cognitive capacities and time frames are very different from those of the adult. In order to protect such children from the potentially devastating effects of discontinuity, we need to better understand the basic developmental processes outlined above and act upon that knowledge so that the child is protected from undue stress.

This chapter is a brief overview of several theories of child development and the tasks that face the young child. Furthermore, it outlines some of the basic issues confronting the child in his quest to accomplish those tasks and some of the conditions necessary for the child to achieve his developmental goals. Finally, developmental concepts are tied to the role that the legal profession can play in facilitating the accomplishment of the child's developmental tasks, when it becomes necessary for the state to become involved and intervene in the family.

FOOTNOTES

1. Jean Piaget, *The Origins of Intelligence in Children*, W. W. Norton and Company, Inc., New York: 1963.

2. John Bowlby, *Attachment and Loss, Vol. 1: Attachment*, Basic Books, New York: 1969; and M.D.S. Ainsworth, "The Development of Infant-Mother Attachment," *The Review of Child Development Research*, Vol. 3, The University of Chicago Press, Chicago: 1973, pp. 1-94.

3. Erik H. Erikson, *Childhood and Society* (2nd ed.), Chapter 7, "The Eight Ages of Man," W. W. Norton and Company, Inc., New York: 1963.

4. Id., p. 270.

5. Joseph Goldstein, Anna Freud, and Albert J. Solnit, *Beyond the Best Interests of the Child*, The Free Press, New York: 1973, p. 42.

SUGGESTED READINGS

Baldwin, Alfred L., *Theories of Child Development,* John Wiley and Sons, Inc., New York: 1968.

Caplan, Frank, *The First Twelve Months of Life,* Grosset and Dunlap, New York: 1973.

Caplan, Frank and Caplan, Theresa, *The Second Twelve Months of Life,* Grosset and Dunlap, New York: 1977.

Caplan, Frank and Caplan, Theresa, *The Early Childhood Years,* Bantam Books, New York: 1983.

Kempe, C. Henry and Helfer, Ray E., *The Battered Child* (3rd ed.), The University of Chicago Press, Chicago: 1980.

Child Abuse and Neglect

THE PEDIATRIC PERSPECTIVE

David L. Kerns, M.D.

The developmental and emotional essence of infancy and childhood is a state of nurturance, safety, stimulation, predictability and unconditional love. It is the one time in our lives when we can and should be cared for without major responsibilities for actively meeting the needs of others. While limits are gradually defined to allow a child to socialize harmoniously within the family, and later in the school setting, on the whole, little is asked and a great deal needs to be given. Parents are entrusted with the difficult and challenging task of providing this fertile environment for a child's healthy development and growth. Sadly, but obviously, the ability to biologically produce a baby is not necessarily coupled with the maturity, love and resources required to meet its needs. At the foundation of all cases of child abuse and neglect is the parental inability—for internal (psychological) and external (stress) reasons—to maintain a developmentally appropriate and enriching environment to which a child, by its very existence, is entitled.

The child's physician is in a unique and strategic position to help parents with the very demanding challenge of parenting and, if need be, to protect children and initiate the rehabilitation of families when a child's rights to safe growth and development are violated at home. Pediatric advocacy for the safety of children in their homes was heralded by the historic description in 1962 of the "Battered-Child Syndrome" by Kempe and his colleagues.[1] Their assertion that child abuse was a frequent cause of disability and death was initially met with a mixed professional response of skepticism by some and energetic mobilization of resources by others. Subsequent incidence studies have indeed validated the magnitude of the problem. The National Center on Child Abuse and Neglect (HEW) estimates that there are nationally approximately one million cases of physical child abuse per year resulting in approximately 2,000 deaths.[2] Gelles, in 1975, examined styles of conflict resolution in a large cross-sectional sample of families and concluded that between 1.4 and 1.9 million children (one out of every 24-33 children) are vulnerable to physical injury at the hands of their parents each year.[3] This striking estimate refers only to physical abuse and does not include the remainder of the spectrum of child abuse and neglect—sexual and emotional abuse and the variety of ways children are neglected.

While compromised socioeconomic status, as a source of many external stresses, may place a family more greatly at risk for abusive and neglectful behavior, the maltreatment of children is by no means exclusively an indigent phenomenon.[4] Surely, reporting patterns significantly obscure the distribution of the problem. The poor family in the "clinic" or "ER" setting is much more likely to be suspected, evaluated and reported than the prosperous family in the private practitioner's office.

Child abuse and neglect exists across social, racial and economic categories and those physicians who "never see it" are not looking well enough. This article describes the various forms of child maltreatment and focuses on the physician's role in diagnosis, decision-making, treatment and prevention.

THE SPECTRUM OF CHILD ABUSE AND NEGLECT

Child abuse and neglect used here interchangeably with maltreatment, refers to a wide variety of damaging caretaker omissions and commissions. While physical and sexual abuse are the most blatant, emotional abuse and the many varied forms of neglect may ultimately be as harmful. Indeed, short of maiming or killing a child, physical abuse takes its developmental and psychological toll through the implicit emotional neglect and abuse accompanying the physical act. The physically abused infant or child is deprived of that precious state of safety, predictability and love which is so crucial for development. With each physical attack comes a message of badness, worthlessness and unlovability. Child abuse and neglect has been very aptly called "the theft of childhood."

Physical abuse, sexual abuse and failure-to-thrive secondary to nutritional neglect will be discussed below in detail.

Emotional abuse is generally synonymous with verbal abuse and refers to a constancy of denigration from parent to child. The young child hears "You are bad," "You're a brat," "You are so stupid," "You can't do anything right," etc. For a young child, reality is the world portrayed by his parents. The verbally abused child will accept that he is bad, stupid, worthless and may be burdened by his low self-esteem and sense of incompetence for a lifetime.

Emotional neglect refers to a lack of loving interaction between parent and child. These children grow up in an affective vacuum. For the preschool child, both affective and cognitive needs are often unmet. Ultimately the impact is the same as in emotional abuse: "Nobody cares for me," "I am unlovable," "I must be bad and worthless."

Physical neglect, i.e., the inability to provide adequate food, shelter, clothing and hygiene, is, of all forms of maltreatment, the most closely related to poverty. The simple lack of resources may make it impossible for the parent to meet middle-class standards of housing, wardrobe and nutrition.

Physical neglect, however, may be a manifestation of other parental issues, especially depression and substance abuse. Frequently, human service professionals will conclude that poor hygiene and marginal clothing indicate poor parenting in a general way. Yet, in indigent populations, many children with inadequate clothing and hygiene are loved and safe in their homes. If a child's appearance is leading to denigration by other children, then it is a real issue, but we should be cautious about what we conclude from appearances alone.

Medical care neglect, particularly noncompliance for immunizations, dental care and illness follow-up, is a common problem for many pediatricians. Occasionally the magnitude of neglect is extreme and will call for aggressive intervention. In dealing with indigent families, it is unrealistic for health care providers to expect health-seeking behavior to be the same as in middle-class populations. Neighborhood and outreach health systems can be instrumental in improving compliance for child care in many poor families.

Supervisional neglect is common, and its impact is primarily expressed in the morbidity and mortality of childhood accidents and poisoning. Most serious accidental injuries and virtually all poisonings are preventable. While any family may experience an occasional accidental injury or ingestion, repeated episodes indicate that parental supervision is inadequate.

Educational neglect refers to either passive collusion with a child's truancy or actual active prevention of a child's school attendance. With rare exceptions in certain religious groups, it is against the law in all states. A subtle form of educational neglect occurs when parent and child are symbiotically tied and mutual resistance to separation keeps the child at home.

Abandonment of a child is a loud and clear message that a parent will not or cannot meet the responsibilities of parenthood. Generally, termination of parental rights follows and the child is freed for adoption.

THE DIAGNOSIS OF PHYSICAL ABUSE, SEXUAL ABUSE AND FAILURE-TO-THRIVE SECONDARY TO CALORIC DEPRIVATION

Physical Abuse

While a refined and integrated social, psychological and developmental assessment of a family is necessary for appropriate intervention in physical abuse cases, the essential first step in diagnosis is a knowledgeable evaluation of physical injuries by the physician. In some instances, e.g., the battered infant, the diagnosis will be self-evident. Often, however, the physical findings alone are ambiguous and diagnosis can only be clarified by the integration of other information about the family members and their environment.

Skin Injuries. Injuries of the skin in various stages of healing are the most common manifestations of physical abuse. Clearly, one must distinguish the very common bumps and bruises of childhood from findings which suggest inflicted trauma. The shins, knees and elbows are the battleground of the healthy, active young child. Bruises and abrasions in these areas should not trigger concern. Nor should an isolated skin lesion which is developmentally and historically consistent with an accidental injury lead to unnecessary exploration for nonaccidental causes.

Of greatest concern are bruises, welts and scars in an infant, injuries to the head and face, and lesions suggesting infliction with an inanimate object such as a belt, cord, hairbrush, etc. Since physical discipline is an accepted and legal parental prerogative in the United States, the physician faces the difficult challenge of developing criteria for what is or is not excessive. I would suggest four guidelines for making these judgments:

■ Infants should never be struck or shaken;
■ Inanimate objects or a closed fist should never be used;

- Slapping should be limited to the extremities and buttocks—never the head, face or perineum;
- Slapping should not be severe enough to injure the skin.

(These guidelines do not indicate the author's approval of physical punishment, but rather are an attempt at defining limits in light of the reality that physical discipline is a common choice of parents.)

Often there is nothing subtle about the bruises on a child. They may be multiple, they may take the form of an inanimate object, they may be developmentally inconsistent with the history given, e.g., that a two-week-old infant rolled off the couch, or they may be simply inadequately explained by any history given, e.g., that multiple facial bruises were sustained by a toddler's fall on a carpeted floor.

When assessing a child with bruises, it is important to perform coagulation screening studies to eliminate the possibility of a bleeding disorder. In correlating histories given with the bruises present on a child, it is necessary to estimate the age of the skin lesions present. Wilson has reviewed the dating of bruises,[5] and his following guidelines may be helpful in determining the age of skin injuries.

1. Initially—red to purple;
2. Within the first week—dark purple;
3. Within the second week—yellow; and,
4. Complete resolution after two to four weeks.

Where there are visible manifestations in a physical abuse case, it is essential to obtain color photographs of the injured areas for possible later use in court proceedings.

Fractures. The finding by radiologists of multiple fractures in various stages of healing[6] and multiple fractures associated with subdural hematomas[7] predated the widespread pediatric recognition of physical child abuse. In infants and children with suspected inflicted injury, a radiologic bone survey may reveal unsuspected healing fracture sites which will confirm the diagnosis of recurrent injury. Occasionally, an infant with failure-to-thrive will also be found to have unsuspected bone injuries.[8] X-rays of long bones, skull, ribs and pelvis should be obtained in all cases of physical abuse and in cases of physical neglect in children under age five.

Fractures of many varieties are seen with physical abuse and those of the long bones and skull are the most common. As with skin injuries, the physician must integrate the clinical picture with the history given by the parents and the developmental capabilities of the child. Accidental fractures in infants are rare—unless they have been accidentally dropped—and multiple distant fractures only occur with catastrophic trauma, e.g., auto accidents. In the latter, all fractures should be in the same stage of repair.

The most common clinically occult finding in a bone survey is the presence of metaphyseal "chip" or "corner" fractures resulting from the violent wrenching or twisting of an extremity. The fresh fracture may be seen or, if the fracture is not new, calcification of a subperiosteal hematoma or later bone remodeling may be apparent. Similar changes, of course, may be seen in the shafts of long bones that are undergoing repair.

Burns. Approximately 10 percent of inflicted injuries to children are burns.[9] Though these occasionally are hard to distinguish from accidental burns, certain patterns have been seen repeatedly. The burning of children with cigarettes, especially on the palms and soles, is a frequent finding. This is a particularly sadistic form of abuse that may indicate a severe psychiatric disturbance in the parent. The lesions are circular and ulcerative and may be in any stage of healing. An accidental brush with a cigarette may cause a superficial burn but should not produce this type of severe, "punched out" lesion. Occasionally, a severely infected insect bite may mimic a cigarette burn.

A second characteristic inflicted burn is the hot water immersion burn or dunking burn. In anger, a parent may plunge and hold a child's arm or leg in scalding hot water. With accidental immersion, a child will withdraw the extremity immediately upon contact with the water and we do not see the severe injury and proximal extent of involvement that occurs with forced immersion. Sometimes, with loss of control in response to toilet training issues, a parent will dunk the child, buttocks and perineum first, into hot water. This creates a characteristic burn pattern with water levels at the thighs and trunk, and possible inclusion of burns to the feet, which may also enter the water.

Head Injuries. The most severe inflicted injuries, in terms of both morbidity and mortality, are head injuries leading to subdural hematomas. While these have in the past been classified as being either related to direct head trauma or spontaneous, it is now clear that the severe shaking of an infant can cause subdural bleeding. The Whiplash-Shaken Infant Syndrome[10] denotes the combination of subdural hematoma and retinal hemorrhages in severely shaken infants who have not had blunt head trauma. These infants will not have skull fractures or any signs of scalp injury. Presently, there is no evidence that spontaneous subdural hematoma is a real entity.

Infants with inflicted head injuries are at great risk for permanent injury to the central nervous system and subsequent fatality. The invocation of "spontaneous subdural hematoma" or "persistent neonatal subdural hematoma secondary to birth injury" (these are virtually always symptomatic in the first hours and days of life) is a grave error which may place a child in serious jeopardy without intervention.

Other Manifestations of Physical Abuse. A wide variety of less common inflicted injuries have been reported in the past several years.[11] These include

1. Retinal injury secondary to thoracic compression (Purtscher Retinopathy);

2. Intentional poisoning;
3. Human bites;
4. Abdominal trauma resulting in hepatic and splenic rupture, intramural bowel hematoma and pancreatic pseudocyst;
5. Genital trauma often related to toilet training;
6. Oral trauma related to forced feeding;
7. Subgaleal hematomas secondary to hair pulling; and
8. Tattooing.

Clues for the Diagnosis of Physical Abuse. While the identification of physical abuse is often clear-cut, just as often the physician faces a seemingly vague and ambiguous picture calling for hard decisions from soft data, a burden shared by all professionals dealing with child abuse and neglect. In such cases, refined history-taking and thoughtful assessment of family functioning will reduce the likelihood of misdiagnosis.

The most consistently validated characteristic of abusive parents is that they themselves were maltreated as children.[12] If not physically abused, they were sexually molested, neglected or experienced discontinuity such as multiple foster placements. Having received these bad messages during childhood, it is not surprising that they often have poor self-esteem coupled with anger and the feeling that they are unlovable. They are unsuccessful in close, lasting relationships, and marital discord, social isolation and the absence of human lifelines are often characteristic. Family crises play an important role in a vulnerable family. The chronic stress of unemployment, health problems, substance abuse and marital disharmony may bring marginal parents to their wit's end. Acute stress, even spilled milk, generally precipitates the actual abusive incident. Particular attention should be given to the stress of a new baby in the household or to a newly discovered pregnancy. While the children of psychotic or sociopathic parents are certainly at great risk, it should be remembered that this group constitutes only approximately 10 percent of all abusive families.[13]

Some children are more vulnerable to physical abuse than
others. Clearly, a happy, cooing, beautiful baby is less likely
to be battered than the irritable, relentless, colicky infant.
Chronic illness, congenital anomalies, and prematurity all place
children more greatly at risk. Perhaps the most vulnerable
child of all is the one who was unwanted in the first place—an
observation that is not only diagnostically relevant but has far-
reaching implications in terms of public policy for sex
education, contraception and abortion.

Abusive parents often have unrealistic expectations of their
children, both developmentally and behaviorally. The infant
who is expected to be toilet trained by six months of age is
indeed in jeopardy. When a child is expected to perform in a
way that is developmentally impossible, he is programmed for
failure, and verbal and physical retribution are likely to follow
leading to continuous erosion of confidence and self-esteem.
Parents who have experienced particularly deprived child-
hoods may turn to their children to meet their never fulfilled
needs for nurturing and dependency (role reversal). An infant
or young child cannot possibly take care of a parent in this
sense and is again set up to fail, disappoint and provoke the
needy parent.

Discrepant histories offered by parents may be helpful
diagnostically. If each parent gives a different explanation for
a child's injuries, it is quite likely that neither explanation is
true. As discussed above, a parent's explanation of an injury
may be developmentally discrepant with the child's motor
capabilities. Delay in seeking medical attention for inflicted
injuries is also a common occurrence among abusive parents.
These families often use multiple health providers in the same
community on an episodic basis, and "doctor-hopping" and
"ER-hopping" are common.

Families in distress will often make medical visits that
superficially are inappropriate. When an upset parent presents
concerns about a child that are quite disproportionate to the
reality of the child's condition, dismissal of the case as "just an
anxious mother" is a serious error. Parents who are mistreat-

ing their children or who are afraid that they will do so may reach out for help in very indirect and inadequate ways. When faced with an over-anxious parent, the physician should directly and supportively ask the parent if there might not be other important issues at home which are really the cause for distress. A multiplicity of inappropriate visits often precedes incidents of physical abuse. The astute clinician has the opportunity in these instances to intervene with services before children are injured.

Sexual Abuse

Over the past few years, the problem of child sexual exploitation, both in the home and for commercial purposes, has become dramatically more visible to professionals as well as to the general public. The incidence of what is considered the last taboo is even more difficult to estimate than that of physical abuse. The American Humane Association estimates that there are 200,000–300,000 cases per year; the National Center on Child Abuse and Neglect (HEW) estimates 60,000–100,000 cases per year;[14] and national extrapolations from the intensive experience in Santa Clara County, California, indicate that there may be as many as 400,000 cases of child sexual abuse per year. These estimates do not include child pornography and prostitution. While discovered extrafamilial assaults, violent or not, are generally reported to law enforcement officials, incest, by far the most common sexual exploitation of children, may be extraordinarily well-concealed for months or even years from anyone outside of the nuclear family.

The impact of sexual abuse on a child may vary from minimal, acute and reversible trauma—as is often the case with a single, nonviolent, heterosexual, extrafamilial episode—to catastrophic developmental and psychological damage wrought by long-term incest. Incest, like emotional and physical abuse, drastically alters the character of childhood.

The child is an instrument of parental needs whose value is measured in parental satisfaction.

Though mother–son, sibling, and homosexual incestuous relationships do occur, the most common are between daughters and fathers (or other adult male figures, e.g., stepfather, maternal boyfriend, uncle, etc.). Some generalizations can be made about chronic father–daughter incest families. Unlike the frequently chaotic, unstable and crisis-ridden physical abuse families, incestuous families are generally very "tight"—they are indeed too tight, locked in a perpetual conspiracy of secrecy, with the daughter's silence and compliance crucial for maintaining a pathologic balance. The mothers are generally withdrawn from both the fathers and daughters. In many cases of chronic incest, the mothers are aware of the sexual activity between father and daughter and they passively or even actively collude in it. At stake for the mother is the maintenance of the family unit. Although the mother has a very weak relationship with the father, family stability meets her dependency needs (often economically) and she essentially sacrifices the daughter to that end. It is not surprising that the daughters are as much or more enraged at their mothers for not having protected them as they are at their fathers for misusing them.

The fathers also tend to be passive and dependent people. Unlike the extrafamilial child molestor, they usually are not pedophiles (people who have a sexual preference for children). They have weak and generally asexual relationships with the mothers, but do not choose to either leave the marriage or seek adult sexual partners outside the marriage. They turn to the daughters out of loneliness and dependency, finding this refuge much less threatening than independence or an extra-marital affair. Generally the sexual activity is affectionate and nonviolent. Unlike rape, which is essentially an act of aggression, the father's incestuous behavior stems from weakness, dependency and loneliness. The sexual activity usually begins with kissing and fondling and progresses over time to masturbation, fellatio, cunnilingus and eventually vaginal intercourse. Generally, vaginal penetration does not take place with very young girls. It is crucial for the physician to keep this in mind since the absence of signs of penetration by no means rules out sexual abuse.

The daughters are caught in the middle of a bizarre family system, functioning to meet the needs of very marginal parents and totally ignoring the developmental and psychological needs of the child. At first the young girl may not perceive that there is anything wrong in the activity. Her father approves and her mother does not intervene. She is told, however, to never tell and never talk about it and senses somehow that something is wrong. She eventually learns that if she ever tells anyone, the whole family may be destroyed. So the daughters are not only exploited sexually and neglected emotionally, but assume the responsibility (and eventually the guilt) for the maintenance of the family unit through sexual compliance and silence.

When disclosure occurs an enormous crisis ensues. The fathers may be jailed, the mothers may deny prior knowledge, and the daughters often face frightening interrogation and examination from a number of strangers. Disclosure may occur in a number of ways. The child may tell a friend, relative, neighbor or teacher. The mother, in an acute crisis with the father, may decide to blow the whistle. Frequently, when the daughters reach adolescence and want to begin dating, the fathers may become very restrictive and protective, preventing the daughters from engaging in a normal, teenage social life. At this point, many daughters, now more influenced by peers than family, will refuse to comply with the fathers and reach out for help.

The physician will be called upon to evaluate a child for suspected sexual abuse either immediately following an extrafamilial assault or following the disclosure of incest. Of course, the physician may be the individual who first learns of an incestuous relationship in the family. As in physical abuse, the family or child may present with veiled complaints, unexplained anxiety or depression or inexplicable behavior problems. The requirements for assessment of child sexual abuse include:

1.   Knowledge of incestuous family dynamics;
2.   Skill in the assessment of family functioning;
3.   Skill in the performance of a pediatric gynecological exam, and
4.   A clear understanding of what constitutes evidence of sexual abuse.

The physician should know that it is likely that he may have both civil and criminal testimonial responsibilities in court as the case progresses. If there is insecurity in these areas, it is appropriate to seek consultation for the child's evaluation.

Interviewing the child or adolescent victim of sexual abuse requires a most patient, gentle and knowledgeable approach. Begin with general inquiries about nonthreatening aspects of school, friends and family. As sensitive information about family relationships emerges, it is crucial that the physician maintain a caring, nonthreatening manner, never communicating surprise, revulsion, or anger. The child's level of anatomic sophistication should be established and the use of vernacular or dolls is often necessary for the clarification of descriptions of sexual activity. If the information given doesn't fit the clinical situation, gently persist or return to the subject matter after a less threatening diversion.

Occasionally, a young child will directly tell us about his or her sexual activities at home. Experience suggests that these allegations by preadolescent children should be taken at face value. While adolescents may fabricate or fantasize sexual episodes with family members, younger children will rarely do so. We have found that a skilled psychologist can be very helpful in distinguishing the angry, aggressive adolescent who is attacking the family by fabricating tales of incest from the actual incest victim. On projective testing, the incest victims see themselves as guilty and threatened and are yearning for a happy, cohesive family; the adolescent who is lying will reveal anger, aggression and withdrawal from the family.

Care should be taken in the preparation of the child for physical examination. Prior explanation of the exam, again using vernacular and/or dolls, should take place. It is crucial that we do not multiply the trauma by "raping" the child in the medical setting with an aggressive, restraining physical assessment.

A physical examination which is medically and legally thorough should include the following:

- *General physical examination.* Pay special attention to signs of physical abuse or neglect.
- *Attention to signs of pregnancy.* Don't miss this one! If there is any question, obtain a urine specimen for a pregnancy test. In Chicago in 1975, approximately 500 eleven-year-olds gave birth to live infants.[15]
- *Inspection of genitalia for signs of trauma.* Bruises, abrasions or lacerations of labial, vaginal, hymenal or anal tissues may be found. Remember, however, that penetration may not have taken place and that does not by any means rule out sexual abuse.
- *Attention to vaginal and rectal foreign bodies.* While it is true that very young children may stick things up themselves, occasionally a perpetrator will insert foreign bodies vaginally or rectally.
- *Perform a venipuncture for VDRL determination and obtain pharyngeal, urethral, vaginal and rectal cultures for gonorrhea.* There has been much controversy in the literature about the mode of transmission of gonorrhea to children. It is clear that the gonorrheal eye disease (ophthalmia neonatorum and conjunctivitis) seen in infants can be transmitted nonvenereally. Several authors[16] have concluded that since no history of sexual contact was elicited in some families where children had clinical nonophthalmic gonorrheal infections, the gonococcal organism could be transmitted nonvenereally to sites other than the eye. From these studies, and from the reluctance to confront the possibility of sexual abuse in families, has grown the belief

that towels, bedsheets, toilet seats, etc. are vectors for this organism. However, in the one study that employed a skilled, experienced and aggressive approach to contact investigation, Branch and Paxton[17] found strikingly different results. Of 20 children with genital gonorrhea in the one-to-four-year age group, 19 had a history of sexual contact; of 25 children with genital gonorrhea in the five-to-nine-year age group, all 25 had a history of sexual contact. All of these children's contacts were in the nuclear or extended family.

While it is not inconceivable that genital gonorrhea could in a rare instance be transmitted nonvenereally, the initial presumption of sexual activity should be made and only after the most experienced investigation has taken place should the possibility of nonvenereal transmission be considered. Acceptance of the mythology of bed sheets and toilet seats removes the physician from a most stressful situation but surrenders the young child to continued sexual activity.

■ *Obtain a vaginal aspirate for microscopic examination for the presence of sperm.*
■ *Note the presence of semen or blood on the clothing or skin of the child.* The clothing can be held as material evidence for judicial proceedings.

The diagnosis of incest is perhaps the most uncomfortable task of pediatrics—but it comes with the job. Sgroi[18] has most aptly written: "Recognition of sexual molestation in a child is entirely dependent on the individual's inherent willingness to entertain the possibility that the condition may exist."

Failure-to-Thrive Secondary to Caloric Deprivation

The term failure-to-thrive (FTT) has frequently been used loosely, encompassing short stature and occasionally incorrectly labeling children who are gaining normally at or just below the third percentile on standardized growth curves.

FTT is a sustained subnormal weight velocity, usually identified in children under three years of age, and significant whether the weight has gone below the third percentile or not. Clinically, we define FTT as a decreased weight velocity resulting in a weight curve that has crossed at least two major percentiles. When infants are calorically malnourished they will have primarily poor weight gain. Their height will be affected only after prolonged caloric deprivation and their brain growth, thus their head circumference, will be affected last. The most common pattern seen in the individual child will therefore be poor weight gain coupled with relatively normal linear and head growth.

In the assessment of weight gain in infancy on a day-to-day basis, the following normal age-specific velocities are helpful: birth to three months—0.9 oz. per day; three to six months— 0.8 oz. per day; six to nine months—0.6 oz. per day, and nine to twelve months—0.4 oz. per day.[19]

The textbook differential diagnosis of FTT is a seemingly endless, and intimidating, list of pediatric diseases—some common, but mostly exotic. Reviews of hospitalized cases reveal an organic etiology in 18–30 percent of the children.[20] The remainder are nonorganic with approximately 50 percent of all cases being due to parental neglect resulting in caloric deprivation.[21] Most nonorganic cases that are not secondary to neglect are due to bona fide technical feeding errors. Occasionally, breastfed babies, with no formula supplements, may gain poorly despite proper technique.[22]

Those infants who are nutritionally neglected by their parents are, no doubt, compromised in terms of their cognitive and affective needs as well. It is, therefore, difficult to know to what extent caloric deprivation per se is detrimental to development. Hertzig studied intelligence in school-age boys who had been severely malnourished in infancy and found their verbal and full-scale IQ scores to be significantly lower than their next elder sibling's.[23] One could argue, however, that perhaps they were more deprived in general than their siblings.

There is much overlap in the characteristics of parents who nutritionally neglect their children and parents who physically abuse them. Indeed, approximately 10 percent of FTT infants are physically abused as well.[24] Mothers of FTT infants are described as dependent, isolated, crisis-ridden and unsupported by fathers. They have often been abused or neglected as children and place their own needs before those of their children. One psychiatric study found a high incidence of character disorders among these mothers[25] and concluded that they were very poor candidates for traditional forms of psychotherapy. No studies to date give a real insight into why some parents physically abuse and others neglect.[26]

Evaluation of FTT infants. The infant who is persistently failing to gain weight adequately at home despite the physician's attempts at nutritional improvement, and who does not have an apparent underlying organic etiology, should be hospitalized. Traditionally, inpatient evaluation has consisted of an elaborate series of laboratory and radiographic studies followed by the consideration of a psychosocial etiology only when all other possibilities are excluded. The fear of missing something, no matter how remote or incongruous with the clinical picture, often takes priority over common sense and reliance on a thorough history and physical examination. R. H. Sills[27] reviewed the hospital evaluations of 185 infants and children with FTT. Of 2,607 studies done, only 36 studies (1.4%) were of positive diagnostic assistance. All 36 studies were specifically indicated by findings on historical or physical examination. There was no positive diagnostic yield (not one test of positive diagnostic assistance!) from studies done in patients whose histories or physicals did not suggest some organic problem.

Occasionally, an FTT infant will enter the hospital with significant dehydration and will require support and parenteral fluids. Most of the time, however, that is not the case. If the admission history and physical examination do not point to an organic etiology, the presumptive diagnosis should be caloric deprivation and the subsequent assessment should focus on the infant's response to a feeding trial, the infant's developmental status, a psychosocial assessment of the family and an assessment of the quality of the parent–infant interaction.

The hospital feeding trial can be fraught with difficulties. These malnourished infants seem to be especially vulnerable to nosocomial infections and their acquisition of gastroenteritis or respiratory symptoms after several days on the ward is common. Often parents will claim that these infants have had diarrhea and/or vomiting at home. Before beginning some special formula in the hospital, a 24-hour observation period with the infant on his usual formula generally reveals the absence of gastrointestinal symptoms. Of course, if the infant is being subjected to repeated procedures, this will also interfere with a valid feeding trial. A calorically deprived infant, placed on a standard 20-calorie-per-ounce formula, given 150–200 calories per kilogram per day, not constantly interrupted by diagnostic procedures, and not burdened by a nosocomial infection, should gain from one to two ounces per day in the hospital. Occasionally, infants with very severe chronic malnutrition will gain more slowly. Rapid weight gain in the hospital is diagnostic of FTT secondary to caloric deprivation. When this diagnosis is established, a radiologic bone survey to rule out occult bone injuries should be ordered.

In the absence of specific historical or physical findings, an extensive, expensive, esoteric organic workup should only be carried out when the feeding trial is unsuccessful and when there are no psychosocial indicators of neglect. The patient who fits these criteria, however, will be rare indeed.

MULTIDISCIPLINARY DECISION-MAKING: CHILD PROTECTION TEAMS

The establishment of a medical diagnosis of child abuse or neglect is one piece of a much larger diagnostic matrix that becomes the basis for a thoughtful dispositional plan for a family. Psychological, socioeconomic, legal and community resource perspectives must be integrated for the development of an appropriate therapeutic approach. No single professional, regardless of his sophistication in his own field, is going to be able to satisfactorily carry out the complex diagnostic and dispositional processes that these cases demand. A child abuse case may require any or all of the following:

- Medical assessment, developmental assessment and psychiatric assessment of the maltreated child and siblings;
- Socioeconomic assessment of the family;
- Psychiatric assessment of the parents;
- Assessment of parent–child interactions by hospital staff;
- Liaison with state or community protective services staff;
- Legal counsel regarding court-related decisions;
- Law enforcement liaison;
- Knowledgeable utilization of community resources; and
- Civil and criminal court testimony by a variety of professionals.

The mechanism that has been developed to meet these needs is the multidisciplinary, multiagency child protection team (CPT). There are hundreds of such teams functioning currently in the United States. Some are hospital-based, some community-based, and some are an integral part of state or county protective services agencies. While the pediatrician need not be the prime mover or the director of a CPT, it is essential that these teams have in their core membership a pediatrician who is knowledgeable and genuinely interested in the management of these cases. CPT's in large communities will generally have the following core membership:

1. Pediatrician;
2. Psychiatrist;
3. Attorney;
4. Medical social worker;
5. Protective services representative;
6. Law enforcement representative; and
7. Public health nurse representative.

In addition, an unlimited variety of personnel become involved on a case-specific basis. In smaller communities, teams consist of combinations of more limited personnel—still far superior to a unidisciplinary approach. Teams meet on a regular basis, generally weekly, and must have the capability to respond to emergencies with ad hoc meetings with at least some of the members. To meet administrative and logistical demands, one individual must function as the coordinator. This responsibility is often rotated among the core members.

The process of CPT case management has been described in great detail by Schmitt.[28] The essential steps are

1. Complete diagnostic assessment of the family;
2. Presentation of diagnostic information to the CPT;
3. Formulation of a diagnostic impression of a family— medical, psychological and socioeconomic;
4. A review of therapeutic and legal alternatives in the community; and
5. Development of an overall plan for treatment and follow-up.

The primary goals of case management are the safety of the child, an acceptable developmental environment for the child, family unity (where the child's safety and development are not compromised), and the provision of services to prevent the recurrence of abusive or neglectful behavior.

The development of an effective multidisciplinary, multi-agency approach faces many obstacles and does not occur overnight. Overcoming territoriality is the greatest challenge. Polarization comes in all varieties: public sector versus private sector, hospital personnel versus nonhospital personnel, social workers versus physicians, etc. The nature of responses to child abuse and neglect dictates that a respectful, trusting and egalitarian team process must develop. In many communities, a schism exists, particularly between protective services workers and hospital personnel, each considering the other naive, incompetent, obnoxious, etc. The families, of course, are the losers in these professional cold wars. The CPT itself serves as the most effective integrator and harmonizer for these rivalries. In the CPT, over time, professionals from different settings get to know one another personally and come to listen well, trust and recognize each other's unique skills. Once everyone realizes that a unidisciplinary approach (regardless of the discipline) is inferior to a multidisciplinary process, territoriality becomes a nonissue. At that point, child maltreatment belongs to the community.

LEGAL RESPONSIBILITIES

Child Protection Laws

All 50 states now have laws which protect children from abusive and neglectful treatment in their homes. Though the statutes vary in some definitions and details, the physician's obligations are fairly consistent throughout the country. Each physician should be familiar with the particular child protection statutes in his or her own state. Reporting known child abuse or neglect, as defined in the individual statutes, is mandatory, and immunity from civil or criminal liability is granted as long as reports are made in good faith. Reports are directed to state or county protective services agencies which are part of the departments of social services or their equivalents. Most states have penalties for nonreporting and civil courts have held that nonreporting may constitute medical malpractice.[29]

Reluctance to reporting is understandable—the confrontation involved is very uncomfortable; the concerns regarding the destruction of a potentially therapeutic relationship with the family are realistic; and the failures of the system to deal with certain families effectively are not infrequent. However, it is not realistic for the physician to believe that he can protect these children and rehabilitate these families without help.

Looking the other way is the worst possible choice, totally ignoring the rights of the child and virtually insuring continued maltreatment and its consequences. Nonreporting does not help the parents or the child. It colludes in the repeated devastation of a child and ultimately to the potential destruction of a family—and—it is against the law.

Interface with Protective Services

Once a physician has initiated a report to protective services, a prompt home visit and psychosocial assessment of a family should be done by a protective services caseworker. This assessment should then be integrated into the dispositional planning of the CPT. The physician has a right to expect a prompt report (at least verbal) from the protective services worker. The protective services agency has the legally mandated authority and responsibility for the ultimate disposition of these cases. It is best when communities are refined to the extent that the difficult decisions are made through the multidisciplinary process.

Being a protective services worker is no picnic—caseloads may be two or three times higher than optimal level (20 cases per worker), training is often inadequate and supervision may be poor. The worker is often caught between angry parents and angry professionals in the community. This is one of the most difficult and thankless jobs in our society and high burnout rates demonstrate this. Physicians and other reporting professionals at times make things even more difficult by setting up the caseworker as a villain—the real bad guy in the system—the child snatcher. By portraying protective services in a negative light, the physician only makes things more painful for the family. His interference delays the healing process, which ought to be a positive outcome. In those difficult moments of confrontation with parents, the messages must be positive: "I am not against you—I am for you and your child;" "I am notifying protective services because I want to help you stop this painful and destructive behavior;" "The role of protective services is to help you and your family to be together in a healthier and safer way."

Court Involvement

Most physicians find the courtroom to be an unfamiliar, time-consuming and threatening place. While the juvenile court is often informal and not particularly stressful for the physician witness, the criminal court can, at times, be a rather brutal experience. In some juvenile court cases, a written medical statement may be adequate, obviating the need for a personal appearance. The use of pediatric consultants for these cases can transfer the testimonial responsibilities to one who is more experienced and comfortable on the witness stand. If you are required to testify, here are a few suggestions which make the experience easier.

1. Know the details of the case thoroughly;
2. Insist that the state or county attorney brief you before-hand on what questions he is going to ask you;
3. Only go to court on call—the court can call you shortly before it is time for your testimony—often hours are spent waiting unnecessarily;
4. Don't yield to an attorney's demands for "yes or no" answers to complex questions—tell the judge that the question cannot be answered simply; and
5. Keep cool, be yourself and don't be intimidated—in most instances the judge will protect you.

Contrary to popular opinion, the court experience can actually be a very positive one—intriguing, educational and therapeutic for the family—if the judges and attorneys are knowledgeable and oriented to a nonpunitive approach.

TREATMENT MODALITIES

Once the diagnostic, dispositional and legal processes have been completed, a comprehensive treatment plan for the family is implemented. No single combination of services can be applied to all families. The specific medical, psychiatric, developmental and socioeconomic needs of each family will determine the particular combination of services offered. Depending on the severity of the case, the child may remain with the family or be in foster placement. The pediatrician's primary responsibility at this point is medical and developmental assessment of the maltreated child and his siblings. Regular visits at much closer intervals than the usual "well child" schedule are appropriate. Continued input to the CPT for follow-up evaluations is necessary. Depending on the size of a community and the refinement of child protection program development, some or all of the following services are available to families.

Alternative Approaches

Traditional psychotherapy and counseling. Though lay therapy and self-help approaches have proven to be the most effective modalities for parents,[30] certain parents will benefit from traditional therapy or counseling. Initial psychiatric evaluations of the parents should determine the appropriate candidates. A minority of the maltreated children will be disturbed to the extent that they need continuing psychiatric care.

Lay Therapy. Many programs nationally now train non-professionals to function as lay therapists (sometimes called Parent Aides) for abusive or neglectful parents. The lay therapists become involved over an extended period of time in the lives of deprived parents, serving as parenting role models (parenting the parents), advisors in household management, liaisons to community agencies and lifelines in times of crisis. A recent study reported that 33 collective years of experience from 11 demonstration projects revealed that of all funded modes of intervention, lay therapy was not only the most effective in terms of low recurrence of maltreatment, but was the most cost effective as well.[31]

Self-Help Approaches. In 1971, the first attempts at application of the self-help model were begun as Mothers Anonymous in California. Since that time there has been a remarkable proliferation of this highly successful approach, now known as Parents Anonymous (PA). At present there are approximately 800 PA chapters in the United States and abroad.[32] PA allows parents to share difficult feelings with other parents in a nonthreatening, nonjudgmental, supportive setting; it provides 24-hour lifelines and combats social isolation for parents; and it allows parents to develop more appropriate expectations of their children's development and behavior. PA has proven to be the most effective of all interventions for child maltreatment with recurrence rates even lower than those with lay therapy clients.[33]

The adaptation of the self-help approach to incest families is known as Parents United.[34] Created in Santa Clara County, California, Parents United chapters are now beginning to proliferate in various parts of the country. These chapters provide the peer approach not only to the incestuous fathers, but to mothers, daughters and sons as well. Like PA, Parents United is very inexpensive and highly effective.

Residential Treatment Facilities. In a few large child abuse and neglect treatment centers, whole family residential treatment has been successful.[35] Though much has been learned through this process which may be very useful in enriching foster care, whole family residential treatment on any large scale is not financially feasible.

Therapeutic Playschool. Though few maltreated children require psychotherapy, the majority have developmental delays, particularly in speech and language areas.[36] In addition, they are frequently distrustful of adults or, if particularly emotionally neglected, indiscriminate in their attachment behavior. Their interactions with other children may be quite antisocial. These children are thus poorly prepared to enter school. High quality preschools with developmentally oriented staff can provide stimulation and socialization for these children.[37]

Enriched Foster Care. The quality of foster care in the United States is uneven at best. While many foster parents are superb, many are mediocre and some are even abusive. The widespread availability of enriched foster care is more a hope for the future than a present-day reality. Some of the approaches to improve foster care are: greater selectivity in the recruitment of foster homes (coupled with higher reimbursement); increased training for foster parents in child development and child care; increased professional supervision of foster parents; and adaptation of the lay therapy concept for foster parent–biologic parent relationships.

Public Health Nurse Home Visitation. Public Health Nurses, with a maternal–child orientation, can be particularly helpful as parent educators in the areas of nutrition, child development, hygiene, discipline, accident and poisoning prevention, and medical compliance. Of all the professional representatives of the system, Public Health Nurses are generally viewed by the parents as the least threatening and the most welcome.

Economic Assistance. In general, the protective services caseworker assumes the responsibility for assisting those parents with financial problems in the acquisition of public assistance, food stamps, WIC (Women, Infants and Children), etc., and for helping them deal with housing and employment issues.

Stress-Relieving Services. Acute and chronic stress are standard ingredients in abusive and neglectful families. While the assumption of domestic tasks by substitutes does not rehabilitate families per se, stress can be reduced to a more tolerable level and the home rendered safer for children and less chaotic for parents.

Many communities now have crisis nurseries available to parents on a drop-in basis 24 hours a day. They provide child care relief often coupled with counseling services for distraught parents. Homemaker's services can provide relief at home and free a parent for increased interaction with his or her children. Likewise, day care can reduce tension in the household and allow the parent to have special time with a particular child.

Substance Abuse Treatment Programs. Substance abuse, particularly alcoholism,[38] plays a significant role in many abusive and neglectful families. Specific intervention programs are essential for the rehabilitation of these families.

Family Planning Services. For those parents who are struggling to keep their family together and to create a safe and loving environment for their children, generally the last thing that is needed is the arrival of a new baby. Easy access to contraceptive services and elective termination of pregnancy is crucial for prevention of further dysfunction in these families. The U.S. Supreme Court decision[39] permitting states to deny Medicaid reimbursement for abortion services may be causing many poor families to bring unwanted children into already chaotic and vulnerable environments.

PRIMARY PREVENTION

Despite the strides that have been made in the diagnosis and treatment of child abuse and neglect in the past two decades, the number of cases is enormous, resources are limited and some families do poorly despite the most vigorous attempts at treatment. The literal cost of child abuse and neglect to society is astronomical. If one child is institutionalized for life because of serious brain injury, the cost will be approximately $700,000.[40] It is becoming increasingly clear that maltreated children are substantially at risk for learning problems,[41] juvenile delinquency,[42] adult criminal behavior,[43] and abusive and neglectful behavior as parents themselves.[44] While efforts at the refinement and expansion of treatment resources are crucial, the development of strategies for the strengthening of families and the primary prevention of maltreatment is equally important. Several approaches to primary prevention are currently being explored.

Enhancement of Parent–Infant Attachment (Bonding)

The very important studies of Klaus and Kennell[45] have shed much light on the process of human parent–infant attachment and have demonstrated that early and extended contact between parents and their newborns has a persisting positive effect on the quality of attachment. Vietze has reported that in a randomly selected population, there was strikingly less child abuse and neglect among families who used "rooming-in" as compared with those families whose infants stayed in the well baby nursery.[46] For those people who bring their own significant vulnerabilities to the beginning of parenthood, it seems that the events of the first minutes, hours and days can make the difference between successful attachment and possible neglect or abuse of their infants.

Klaus and Kennell have recommended a number of perinatal routines which can serve to enhance parent–infant bonding.[47]

1. An individualized assessment should be made of each family's needs and desires relating to the birth experience and the new infant;
2. Prenatal preparation should be provided which includes education regarding labor, delivery and newborns, prepa-

ration for labor, e.g., LaMaze classes, and tours of the
obstetrical and newborn facilities;

3. A specific person, preferably the prospective father, should
be with the mother throughout the birthing process;

4. Eye medication (silver nitrate) should be delayed until
approximately one hour of age to allow the parents to
experience reciprocal eye-to-eye contact while the infant is
in the quiet alert state;

5. If the mother and the newborn are well, they and the father
should be allowed to interact alone for the 30–45 minutes
before the beginning of the infant's first nap;

6. Rooming-in should be available and encouraged for all
well mothers with well newborns; and

7. Family visiting should be unlimited and strongly
encouraged.

All family members benefit from the mutual support and
intimacy of this special time.

A healthy childbirth is really a social event—a family event.
The progress that has been made in the prevention of
infectious complications and reduction of maternal and infant
mortality has also had the negative effect of "medicalizing"
childbirth. The operating room ambiance, excessive anesthesia
and analgesia, and unnecessary maternal–infant separations all
contribute to making childbirth a sickness-like experience for
the family. It would be nice to think that the current
movement toward family-centered obstetrics is an expression
of a widespread perception by the medical profession that the
family's needs are not being fully met. In fact, the trend
toward demedicalization of the birthing experience has been
more an outgrowth of the woman's movement, the consumer
movement, and a good deal of common sense on the part of
families. It is clear that childbirth can be a social event without
compromising medical care. Today's hospital-based, family-
centered perinatal units are fully able to enhance family
attachments and provide high-quality medical interventions
for mothers and infants when necessary.

Early Identification of Families in Need of Services

Child abuse and neglect do not occur unexpectedly in families that are functioning well. The many antecedents that have been described are apparent if those that are involved with the families are focused and observant. Gray, et al., have conducted a perinatal assessment study which has demonstrated the ability to identify high-risk families and further, that intervention in these families prevented maltreatment when compared with high-risk nonintervention families.[48] Particularly predictive were labor and delivery room observations which focused on: How does the mother look? What does the mother say? and What does the mother do?

In the primary care setting, the pediatrician has the ideal opportunity to identify vulnerable families early and refer them for appropriate services. Prior to school, the doctor's office is the only place in our society through which children and families pass en masse. Pediatricians need to get to know their families in a way that goes well beyond the yield of the routine family history. The tactful and supportive exploration of details of family functioning can legitimatize the doctor's office as a place where parents can get attention and support for problems before children get hurt. The pediatrician needs to know about the quality of marital relationships, disciplinary styles, economic stresses, substance abuse and emotional problems within the homes of his patients. True preventive pediatrics must include a real assessment of the child's family environment. The routine assessment of family functioning takes some extra time and calls upon communication skills that have generally not been taught in medical school or pediatric residency training. However, the tactful, caring physician will find that most parents are willing to discuss problems at home and reach out for help.

Education for Parenthood

Though virtually any parent will tell you that child-rearing is one of the most difficult tasks in life, little attention is paid to the education of young people in this area. Often new parents know very little about infant health and almost nothing about child development and behavior. I would speculate that naivete about the realities of parenting and single, teenage pregnancy are quite related.

Our school systems are a nearly untapped resource for education for parenthood. Though most high schools have elective courses in child development, there is generally no skill-training in child care, almost all of the students are females, and teachers will tell you that the students who elect these courses are the very ones who need them the least. Mandatory courses in child care and development in our schools could be a substantial contribution to the primary prevention of child abuse and neglect. Creative model curricula have been developed,[49] some incorporating day care centers and nursery schools physically within the high school settings.

Most hospitals have some form of prenatal classes which generally focus on having a baby, rather than on being a parent. The hospital, with a relatively captured population, should, on an individual and group basis, develop high quality parent education programs in both the obstetrical and pediatric settings. There should be flexibility for educational level and ethnic content, and child development and behavior should be emphasized.

Health Visitors

In general, Public Health Nurses are called upon as a resource to families only after difficulties at home are recognized. However, the need for education and support to new parents is so widespread that routine health visitation has become standard procedure in several Western European countries and is now being piloted in a number of settings in the United States. Manpower limitations have led to the use of trained paraprofessionals—Lay Health Visitors—in this role.

The Health Visitor is essentially a maternal–child public health nurse aide, visiting new parents at home and focusing on education in child development, behavior, nutrition, hygiene, discipline, accident prevention and medical compliance. The Health Visitor is capable of family functioning assessment and is able to identify families that are at risk for harmful child-rearing practices.[50]

Preliminary data from the program at Colorado General Hospital demonstrate a decreased incidence of child abuse and neglect in the population served.[51] The widespread implementation of routine home visitation programs which are oriented to health and prevention may be a reality in the future. In the meantime, pediatricians should make abundant use of the services of public health and visiting nurse programs in their communities. These services are often quite underutilized and called upon only after families are in a great deal of trouble.

THE PEDIATRICIAN'S ROLE

As child abuse and neglect become more visible, and as communities develop increasingly sophisticated programs, the pediatrician's involvement in prevention, diagnosis and management becomes more widespread and frequent. Some of the knowledge and skills required have often not been acquired in medical school or residency: physical assessment of abuse; assessment of family functioning; court testimony; and utilization of community resources. Involvement in the cases is often time-consuming and emotionally draining. The group decision-making process of the Child Protection Team asks the pediatrician to function as an egalitarian peer with a number of other human service professionals. This is in contrast to the traditional medical hierarchy which places the physician in a distinctly authoritative position. This political transition may be difficult not only for the physician but for the former subordinates as well.

Personal attitudes, prior training, time constraints and the availability of local expertise will determine the degree to which a given pediatrician will become involved. Some will choose to refer all cases to a local pediatric subspecialist. Many will remain the managing physician throughout the case with the use of consultants. Finally, some will become extensively involved with child protection teams and community child protection counsels, will serve as consultants and will be instrumental in program development and child advocacy as well as individual case management. The minimum requirements for any pediatrician are

1. Skill in the physical assessment of the full spectrum of child abuse and neglect;
2. Skill in the assessment of child development and family functioning;
3. Knowlege of child protection legal responsibilities; and
4. Sophistication in the utilization of community resources.

The child who is in danger emotionally and/or physically at home deserves skillful intervention by his physician. In moving into the areas of child protection and family rehabilitation, many pediatricians are exploring virgin territory. However, the appropriate knowledge and skills are available, the legal framework is in place, and prevention and treatment resources are becoming increasingly effective and proliferated. Child abuse and neglect are upsetting, but so are cancer, cystic fibrosis and chronic renal disease. Of these, maltreatment is the most common and the most curable. Once past the initial unfamiliarity and discomfort of working with dysfunctional families, the pediatrician will find his involvement challenging and, in most instances, rewarding as children are allowed to grow and develop in safer, more enriching environments.

FOOTNOTES

1. C. Henry Kempe, F. Silverman, B. F. Steele, et al, "The Battered Child Syndrome," *Journal of the American Medical Association* 181:17, 1962.

2. Douglas J. Besharov, *Federal Standards for Child Abuse and Neglect Prevention and Treatment Programs and Projects (Draft)*, Department of Health, Education and Welfare, Washington, D.C., 1978, p. xi.

Note: The National Center on Child Abuse and Neglect (now Health and Human Services) reports that in 1983 there were 1,007,658 official reports of child abuse and neglect. This number of reports represents an estimated 1.5 million children.

3. R. J. Gelles, "Violence Toward Children in the United States," *American Journal of Orthopsychiatry* 48:580, 1978.

4. Douglas J. Besharov and P. B. Duryea, "Report on the New York State Assembly State Committee on Child Abuse," in *The Battered Child,* (1st ed.) Ray E. Helfer and C. Henry Kempe (eds.), University of Chicago Press, Chicago: 1968.

5. E. F. Wilson, "Estimation of the Age of Cutaneous Contusions in Child Abuse," *Pediatrics* 60:750, 1977.

6. F. Silverman, "The Roentgen Manifestations of Unrecognized Skeletal Trauma in Infants," *American Journal of Roentgenology* 69:413, 1953.

7. J. Caffey, "Multiple Fractures in Long Bones of Infants Suffering from Chronic Subdural Hematoma," *American Journal of Roentgenology* 56:163, 1946.

8. K. Vedder and E. Zieserl, "The Positive Value of the Skeletal Survey in Child Abuse and Neglect," *Ambulatory Pediatric Association Abstracts,* 1974, p. 35.

9. R. W. Gillespie, "The Battered Child Syndrome: Thermal and Caustic Manifestations," *Journal of Trauma* 5:523, 1965.

10. J. Caffey, "On the Theory and Practice of Shaking Infants," *American Journal of Diseases of Children* 124:161, 1972.

11. C. Henry Kempe, "Uncommon Manifestations of the Battered Child Syndrome," *American Journal of Diseases of Children* 129:1265, 1975.

12. B. F. Steele and C. B. Pollock, "A Psychiatric Study of Parents Who Abuse Infants and Small Children," in *The Battered Child,* (1st ed.) Ray E. Helfer and C. Henry Kempe (eds.), University of Chicago Press, Chicago: 1968, p. 226.

13. Id.

14. The National Center on Child Abuse and Neglect reports that in 1983 there were over 90,000 official reports of sexual abuse, representing an estimated 130,000 children.

15. S. M. Sgroi, "Comprehensive Examination for Child Sexual Assault: Diagnostic, Therapeutic and Child Protection Issues," in *Sexual Assault of*

Children and Adolescents, Ann W. Burgess, et al (eds.), Lexington Books, Lexington, MA.: 1978, p. 145.

16. B. Michalowski, "Difficulties in Diagnosis and Treatment of Gonorrhea in Young Girls," *British Journal of Venereal Diseases* 37:142, 1961; W. W. Tunnesen, and Jastremske: "Prepubescent Gonococcal Vulvo-Vaginitis," *Clinical Pediatrics* 13:675, 1974; and W. B. Shore and J. A. Winkelstein, "Non-Venereal Transmission of Gonococcal Infections to Children," *Journal of Pediatrics* 79:661, 1971.

17. G. Branch and R. Paxton, "A Study of Gonococcal Infections Among Infants and Children," *Public Health Reports* 80:347, 1965.

18. S. M. Sgroi, "Sexual Molestation of Children," *Children Today* 4(3):18, 1975.

19. Barton D. Schmitt and C. Henry Kempe, "The Pediatrician's Role in Child Abuse and Neglect," *Current Problems in Pediatrics,* Yearbook Medical Publishers, 5(5), Chicago, 1975, p. 19.

20. Barton D. Schmitt and C. Henry Kempe, *supra* note 19; and R. H. Sills, "Failure-to-Thrive: The Role of Clinical and Laboratory Evaluation," *American Journal of Diseases of Children* 132:967, 1978.

21. Id.

22. P. A. O'Connor, "Failure-to-Thrive with Breast Feeding," *Clinical Pediatrics* 17:833, 1978.

23. M. E. Hertzig, M. G. Birch, S. A. Richardson, et al, "Intellectual Levels of School Children Severely Malnourished During the First Two Years of Life," *Pediatrics* 49:814, 1972.

24. Barton D. Schmitt and C. Henry Kempe, *supra* note 19.

25. J. Fischoff, C. F. Whitten, and M. G. Pettit, "A Psychiatric Study of Mothers of Infants with Growth Failure Secondary to Maternal Deprivation," *Journal of Pediatrics* 79:209, 1971.

26. For further information on failure-to-thrive, see the following recent articles: E. Seigel, "A Critical Examination of Maternal-Infant Bonding Its Potential for the Reduction of Child Abuse and Neglect," in *Child Abuse, A Community Concern,* K. Oates (ed.), Bruner/Mazel, New York: 1982; and C. F. Haynes, C. Cutler, J. Gray and Ruth S. Kempe, "Hospitalized Cases of Non-Organic Failure-to-Thrive: The Scope of the Problem and Short-Term Lay Health Visitor Intervention," *Child Abuse and Neglect,* Special Edition, 8:229 (1984).

27. R. H. Sills, *supra* note 20.

28. Barton D. Schmitt (ed.), *The Child Protection Team Handbook,* Garland Press, New York: 1978.

29. See, e.g., *Landeros v. Flood,* 131 Cal Rptr 69, 551 P.2d 389 (1976).

30. *Evaluation of the Joint OCD/SRS National Demonstration Program in Child Abuse and Neglect, Executive Summary,* Berkeley Planning Associates for the National Center for Health Services Research (DHEW), 1977.

31. Id.

32. *Note:* According to the Parents Anonymous office, in 1986 there were 1,200 PA chapters nationally and in a few foreign countries.

33. *Evaluation, supra,* note 30.

34. H. Giarretto, "Humanistic Treatment of Father-Daughter Incest," in *Child Abuse and Neglect: The Family and the Community,* Ray E. Helfer and C. Henry Kempe (eds.), Ballinger, Cambridge, MA.: 1976, p. 143.

35. H. Alexander, Mary McQuiston and M. Rodeheffer, "Residential Family Therapy," in *The Abused Child: A Multidisciplinary Approach to Developmental Issues and Treatment,* Harold P. Martin (ed.), Ballinger, Cambridge, MA.: 1976, p. 235; and V. J. Fontana and E. Robison, "A Multidisciplinary Approach to the Treatment of Child Abuse," *Pediatrics* 57:760, 1976.

36. F. Blager and Harold P. Martin, "Speech and Language of Abused Children," in *The Abused Child: A Multidisciplinary Approach to Developmental Issues and Treatment,* Harold P. Martin (ed.), Ballinger, Cambridge, MA.: 1976, p. 83.

37. J. Mirandy, "Preschool for Abused Children," in *The Abused Child: A Multidisciplinary Approach to Developmental Issues and Treatment,* Harold P. Martin (ed.), Ballinger, Cambridge, MA.: 1976, p. 215.

38. D. W. Behling, "Alcohol Abuse as Encountered in 51 Instances of Reported Child Abuse," *Clinical Pediatrics* 18:87, 1979.

39. *Maher v. Roe,* 432 U.S. 464, 97 S.Ct 2476 (1977).

40. C. Henry Kempe, "Approaches to Preventing Child Abuse: The Health Visitors Concept," *American Journal of Diseases of Children* 130:941, 1976.

41. Harold P. Martin and M. Rodeheffer, "Learning and Intelligence," in *The Abused Child: A Multidisciplinary Approach to Developmental Issues and Treatment,* Harold P. Martin (ed.), Ballinger, Cambridge, MA.: 1976, p. 93.

42. J. Alfaro, "Report of the New York State Assembly Select Committee on Child Abuse," *Child Protection Report* II:1:1, Washington, D.C., 1976.

43. E. Tanay, "Psychiatric Study of Homicide," *American Journal of Psychiatry* 125:1252, 1969.

44. B. F. Steele and C. B. Pollock, *supra* note 12.

45. Marshall H. Klaus and John H. Kenell (eds.), *Maternal-Infant Bonding,* C. V. Mosby, St. Louis: 1976.

46. P. M. Vietze, "The Effect of Extended Contact on Mothering Disorders: A Controlled Study of 500 Families," presented to the *Parent-to-Infant Attachment Conference,* Cleveland, Ohio, November, 1977.

47. Marshall H. Klaus and John H. Kenell, *supra* note 45.

48. J. Gray, C. Cutler, J. Dean, et al, "Prediction and Prevention of Child Abuse," *Pediatric Research* 10:103, 1976.

49. Elizabeth Ogg, *Preparing Tomorrow's Parents*, Public Affairs Committee, New York, 1975.

50. C. Henry Kempe, *supra* note 40.

51. Personal communication, C. Henry Kempe.

Note: See, J. Gray and B. Kaplan, "The Lay Health Visitor Program: An Eighteen-Month Experience," in *The Battered Child* (3rd ed.), C. Henry Kempe and Ray E. Helfer (eds.), University of Chicago Press, Chicago: 1980.

THE ROLE OF THE SOCIAL WORKER

Judith C. White, M.A.

The social worker may come into contact with the abused or neglected child in a variety of settings. These include hospitals, schools, private agencies which are treatment-oriented, and public agencies which are legally responsible for provision of services to families with children in need of protection. This chapter discusses the role of the social worker who works in the public agency setting.

When dealing with families who have come to an agency's attention because of suspected abuse or neglect, the protective services worker is placed in an unusual and often difficult position. She is there to protect the child (and represents the authority to take the child away), but also to offer or provide services to the family so that the necessary changes can occur. This dual role of watchdog/advocate seemingly would create an untenable situation, but, in fact, most protective services workers do maintain an effective relationship with the families on their caseloads. The worker's attitude serves as the foundation for this relationship. Although the prevailing community attitude toward abusive or neglectful parents is often anger and a wish for punishment, the social worker must remain nonjudgmental if she is to establish rapport with these parents. It is important for her to believe and to communicate to her clients that almost anyone in a stressful enough situation is capable of abusing his/her children. This is not to say that such behavior is excused, but the line between discipline and abuse can become quite turbid. However, to be workable, the parent must be able to recognize that certain behavior has exceeded this boundary, and make the adjustments necessary to provide minimally adequate care for the child.

There are several distinct phases of casework in which the protective services worker is involved: Assessment, Protection of the Child(ren), Coordination, Treatment and the Court Process.

ASSESSMENT

Assessment is an ongoing process that begins the moment a report of child abuse or neglect is received and continues throughout each of the subsequent phases of casework. The responsibilities were well stated by Florence Hollis.

> The most significant contribution and primary responsibility of the social worker is the social work assessment, i.e., the process of making a psychosocial diagnosis. In doing this, the social worker collects data, evaluates it, orders data into a diagnosis and determines a treatment plan.[1]

When assessing the abusive or neglectful family, the initial assessment may be conducted under less than ideal circumstances. Because reports alleging injury, serious neglect or dangerous environment to a child must be investigated immediately and the parents are often the unwilling and hostile subjects of these reports, information gained from the first contact with a family may be quite skewed. On the other hand, the family members are in a crisis position during the initial investigation, with their defenses down and may reveal an abundance of valuable information before they have again mobilized defenses. Awareness of the worker's authority to remove their children can cause some typically resistant parents to be, at least temporarily, revealing and cooperative.

The primary result of the immediate psychosocial assessment following a report of abuse or neglect, must be a determination of the safety of the child or children in the home. Can protection be accomplished without disruption of the family unit or must the children be temporarily removed for their own safety? In making this (sometimes on the spot) decision, a worker should rely on a combination of intuition, understanding of child development, and a knowledge of the high-risk factors or "red flags" present in abusive or neglectful families.

- A failure to understand and recognize the normal capabilities of children.
- The reversal of the parent/child role, i.e., the child is responsible for the emotional and sometimes physical needs of the parent. The child's needs are secondary and he/she is viewed as a source of parental gratification.
- A high expectation for obedience and a belief that excessive punishment is justifiable, e.g., "My mother whipped me and I deserved it."
- The parent's history of an abusive childhood. This is a key since we know that parents will usually parent the way they were parented.
- Social isolation which is indicated by few or poor relationships and a lack of personal and community supports.

The worker also needs to consider that removing the child always alters the family dynamics. The child's role as scapegoat or source of gratification is an important part of the family's functioning, however unhealthy. Therefore, the worker responsible for removal is often viewed as a depriver.

Since the initial contacts with a family occur under such stressful conditions, especially if a child has been removed, it may be helpful to assign one worker to perform the intake or initial assessment and another to perform the ongoing duties.

It is not easy to be warm and suspicious at the same time. Where agency size and organization permit, this division of responsibility can allow the family members to focus their hostility onto the intake worker. She is viewed as the punitive one who unjustly invaded their domain and disrupted their lives. The ongoing worker, then, can build a relationship with the family for the expressed purpose of working jointly toward alleviating the factors which threaten the child's welfare.

When the questions regarding a child's immediate safety have been answered, the protective services worker can move on to other areas of assessment. A complete social history of the family should include: parents' functioning (childhood and current), child's functioning, family interaction and environmental stresses. The collection and evaluation of this information is a focus of the early phases of the worker–family relationship, but it cannot be overemphasized that assessment is a process of gradual unfolding and the treatment plan must always be flexible enough to accommodate new information.

A worker cannot expect to thoroughly know a family in a month or two, even though she's required to develop a treatment plan within that time frame. Every worker has known one family that she thought she had pegged, only to learn that they had been hiding some crucial piece of family history for months or years.

PROTECTION OF THE CHILD

The safety of the child must remain the overriding concern throughout the casework relationship with the abusive or neglectful family. If this tenet is ever in conflict with the treatment or preservation of a family unit, the child's need for protection must always take precedence. It is often assumed that safety is only a concern as long as the child remains in his/her own home. However, there are concerns with foster care too, such as the trauma of separation and the risk of abuse by the foster family.

COORDINATION

It is absolutely essential to good social work for the worker to view herself as a member of a team, the configuration of which will change with each case. No single professional can provide the abusive or neglectful family with all the services necessary to reorganize itself, nor should the complicated and delicate issues of child protection be made the domain of any one discipline. The protective services worker, though, is expected to be the coordinating or managing force behind the team of professionals, paraprofessionals and family members brought together for the purpose of treating the family and protecting the child. While the law and agency policy dictate some of the professionals with whom she will work on a case, the social worker retains a certain amount of freedom to choose the other participants. The protective services worker is most likely to collaborate with: attorneys, physicians, mental health professionals, school and daycare personnel, foster parents, family members, law enforcement officials and lay therapists (e.g., parent aides).

TREATMENT

In determining a treatment plan for a family, there are several elements and issues that must be considered by the protective services worker. The worker must remain aware of some of the emotional pitfalls of the treatment phase of the casework process, keep a broad perspective of the total picture and organize her plan accordingly. It is easy to feel overwhelmed by the apparent disorganization and dysfunction of many of the families that come to the attention of protective services. The seemingly impossible task of reorganizing a parent's personality, which is stuck at an immature level of development and apparently can only be remedied by complete reparenting, is enough to make the most dedicated social worker consider a career change. In executing a course of treatment for a family, the worker can expect to be emotionally attacked, rejected and thwarted by her clients. She must remember, however, that this is not a personal attack, but rather reflects the client's view of an unfriendly world. The worker's ability to skillfully reduce expectations of her clients while maintaining a view of their potential, to hold the clients in high esteem and to meet the needs of clients so that they, in turn, can meet the needs of their children, will go a long way in facilitating the treatment process. The abusive or neglectful parent usually has a long history of excessive demands being placed on him/her and resulting numerous failures. The effective worker is wise to avoid contributing to this pattern.

The design of a treatment plan for an abusive or neglectful family is dictated by an individual family's needs, the available resources and the belief that the purpose of treatment is to facilitate change in the areas of a family's life that directly or indirectly affect the parent's ability to physically care for or be emotionally available to the child. An example of such a treatment plan might be better impulse control, improved patterns of discipline, or more reasonable expectations of the child. Davoren in *The Battered Child* writes

> A change for the better that could be counted on, that would not easily be reversed, has usually been preceded or accompanied by a marked improvement in the family's economic stability—no matter how economically successful the family had been originally.[2]

Other considerations that may help formulate the treatment plan include special needs of the child (e.g., medical or educational), mental health needs of parents and concrete needs of the family (e.g., housing, food or medical care). Some of the agency and community resources available to fill these needs might be

- ■ *Placement.* Includes foster care, residential care and protective day care. This can temporarily reduce family stress, ensure the safety of the child and provide therapy for the child and parents (in some therapeutic foster care settings or residential treatment facilities). Additionally, placement of a child out of the home can be a tremendous motivating factor for previously noncompliant parents.
- ■ *Mental Health Counseling.* With a psychiatrist, psychologist or social worker; individual, marital or family; through private individuals, agencies, hospitals or community mental health centers. Here is an area where ongoing assessment comes into play in the form of the psychiatric or psychological evaluation.
- ■ *Parent Education.* Can be provided from within the child protection agency or from the community. The particular course or class should be appropriate to an individual client's level of intellectual functioning, should be sensitive to cultural issues and should include information on child development and the dynamics of abuse and neglect.
- ■ *Agency and Community Support Staff.* Includes homemakers, parent aides, Big Brothers/Sisters, visiting nurses, etc.
- ■ *Support Groups.* Self-help groups for parents (e.g., Parents Anonymous) and children (e.g., Daughters United).

In choosing resources and implementing the treatment plan, the worker must keep a clear focus on the following elements: monitoring behavior change in the abuser, helping the family to manage stress and encouraging the family's strengths so as to ensure the child's safety and well-being. Some of the healthy signs of change the protective services worker delights in seeing are a development in the parent of a positive self-image, a capacity for compassion, a capacity for true friendship and a lack of jealousy or feeling threatened by others' attention to the child or the child's attention to others.

Occasionally, situations arise that appear to seriously hinder the success of a treatment plan. One of these is the occurrence of further abuse or neglect that the social worker is obligated to report. When this happens, the worker again may be placed in the dual role of reporting (or investigative) agent and treatment agent. The reporting of the incident or the subsequent removal of the child may permanently damage the worker–family relationship. If this happens, the worker may want to consider shifting the major responsibility for treatment to another agency or professional. If the alliance is completely destroyed, the case may have to be transferred to a new social worker.

Another situation that may appear at first glance to impede the progress of a course of treatment is a turnover in agency personnel. While the new worker on a case may need some orientation and relationship-building time, she may also bring to the case a fresh perspective and new reserves of energy and patience, and may ultimately be the more effective worker. This may be likened to one parent taking over the second shift with a difficult or sleepless child, after the other parent is exhausted.

COURT

Although the civil court action in abuse and neglect cases is not designed to be adversarial, in reality it is experienced that way by most parents. The feelings this engenders range from anger and aggression to fear and intimidation. The combination of angry and hostile parents who feel powerless to begin with and the impossible demands (from the parent's perspective) made by the court create some special challenges for the protective services worker. Again, the worker may feel herself to be in a difficult position. She is the one required to make treatment and placement recommendations to the court which will, in turn, become orders of the court; yet she is also expected by the court to assist the family in carrying out these orders.

Even though the intent of the law is to preserve families, few who are the subject of a dependency and neglect court action are able to be convinced of that. They see, instead, only the short-term consequences of the court's involvement, which is viewed more as interference, e.g., removal of children, loss of time from work and more impossible demands. In order to neutralize what can easily become more reinforcement for the client's hostile and punitive view of the world, the social worker's role in the court process needs to be that of an interpreter, in addition to formulator of the treatment plan. It can encourage cooperation and reduce resistance if the worker explains at the outset, and in simple language, the various steps of the process, the possible outcomes, the client's alternatives and responsibilities and areas where he/she may influence the outcome. Cooperation may be additionally elicited by helping the client to plan for the time off required by the various hearings and by sincerely soliciting and utilizing his/her feedback in developing the treatment plan, e.g., "What special help do you think Lisa needs?"

The role of the social worker involved with the abusive or neglectful family is a multifaceted one. It requires knowledge, patience, a strong self-image, flexibility, an empathic attitude toward the client and a willingness to collaborate with a variety of professionals who each support the goal of positive family change and protection of the child.

FOOTNOTES

1. F. Hollis, "Diagnosis" (Chapter XI), *Casework: A Psychological Therapy,* Random House, New York: 1964.

2. E. Davoren, "The Role of the Social Worker," in *The Battered Child* (1st ed.), Ray E. Helfer and C. Henry Kempe (eds.), University of Chicago Press, Chicago: 1968.

DEFINING CHILD ABUSE AND NEGLECT FROM A LEGAL PERSPECTIVE

Donald C. Bross, J.D., Ph.D

The many different kinds of law use varied definitions of child abuse and neglect. Criminal charges, dissolutions of marriage, dependency and neglect petitions, tort claims and other forms of legal proceedings are undertaken for different purposes, even though harm to a child can be an issue in each type of law. Advocates for children must understand the varying uses of each type of law for the purposes of child protection, and the differing requirements needed to make a legal determination that child abuse or neglect has occurred. In keeping with our purposes, however, the definition of child abuse and neglect in civil, state child protection proceedings will be the primary focus of this discussion.

DIFFERENT PURPOSES FOR DEFINING CHILD ABUSE AND NEGLECT

Among the reasons for defining child abuse and neglect are to assist us in understanding when abuse or neglect should be reported, when a report should be administratively substantiated by child protective services, when abuse or neglect can be adjudicated and when, in criminal proceedings only, a specific defendant can be convicted of a crime of child abuse. It is essential to remember the purposes of these different activities to avoid confusion about what can be reasonably construed as abuse or neglect.

Reporting

From an epidemiological perspective, reporting of a disease or other condition that needs to be controlled for the public and individual good should sweep a broad net for possible cases. Any suspected case should be reported for professional evaluation, if the condition or conduct over which control is sought is dangerous enough, and/or if it is hard to confirm or rule out without professional experience and training. In all 50 of the United States the child abuse reporting laws are fairly broad. State reporting statutes reflect the difficulty of knowing when children, often isolated from society and inherently vulnerable because of age, are not receiving minimal care.

The varied U.S. reporting laws have many similarities, in part because the laws were first enacted in all 50 states between 1963 and 1967,[1] and, in part, because the federal government provides support, on the condition that certain minimal standards for state reporting laws on child protection are met.[2] The Model Child Protection Act proposed by the Department of Health, Education and Welfare in 1977[3] contains elements common to the greatest majority of state reporting laws.

(a) "Child" means a person under the age of 18.
(b) An "abused or neglected" child means a child whose physical or mental health or welfare is harmed or threatened with harm by the acts or omissions of his parent or other person responsible for his welfare.
(c) "Harm" to a child's health or welfare can occur when the parent or other person responsible for his welfare:
    (i) inflicts or allows to be inflicted, upon the child, physical or mental injury, including injuries sus-

           tained as a result of excessive corporal punishment; or,

(ii)   commits, or allows to be committed, against the child a sexual offense, as defined by state law; or,

(iii) fails to supply the child with adequate food, clothing, shelter, education (as defined by state law), or health care, though financially able to do so, or offered financial or other reasonable means to do so; for the purposes of this Act, "adequate health care" includes any medical or non-medical remedial health care permitted or authorized under state law; or,

(iv) abandons the child as defined by state law; or,

(v)   fails to provide the child with adequate care, supervision or guardianship by specific acts or omissions of a similarly serious nature requiring intervention of the child protective service or a court.

(d)   "Threatened harm" means a substantial risk of harm.

(e)   "A person responsible for a child's welfare" includes the child's parent, guardian, foster parent, an employee of a public or private residential home, institution or agency; or the person legally responsible for the child's welfare in a residential setting.

(f)   "Physical injury" means death, or permanent or temporary disfigurement or impairment of any bodily organ.

(g)   "Mental injury" means an injury to the intellectual or psychological capacity of a child as evidenced by an observable, substantial impairment in his ability to function within his normal range of performance and behavior, with due regard to his culture.[4]

While these elements are common to most state reporting statutes, each state varies enough that wording may be very significant in a given situation.[5] Thus, the conviction of a psychiatrist who failed to report that his adult patient's daughter was being sexually abused by the patient, was overturned on the basis of the statute (which has since been amended) that required reporting only by those individuals "serving children."[6]

No matter how similar or different, however, these definitions of abuse and neglect leave much unclear. Are skin bruises "impairment of a bodily organ"? Does it matter whether the bruises are on the buttocks or on the face, and whether the child is six months, six years or sixteen years of age? It is important for the reporting individual to know that merely *suspected* cases may be reported, and must be reported if the individual is a mandated reporter. Still, the substantiation by social services and adjudication in the courts involves a review of much detail about the child, parents and overall situation. The process uses the framework of written definition, but is itself also essential to defining child abuse and neglect. In other words, what do reasonable physicians, social workers, judges, jurors and, in general, the community consider to be unacceptable levels of various harms and risks of harm to children?

Substantiation versus Probable Cause

Social workers trying to decide if a case should be "substantiated" have different standards than a prosecutor trying to determine if there is "probable cause" for criminal charges. Each discipline tries to anticipate, in part, how a court might respond to a case. This is a useful check and balance on one's own judgment. Court action is not the only alternative being weighed, however. The prosecuting attorney also thinks of plea bargains, deferred judgments and deferred sentences, as well as dismissing charges already filed with or without prejudice. The social worker considers voluntary services, voluntary written agreements, deferred filing, continued adjudication and a conclusion that a case is unfounded. The degree to which the facts of an individual case meets the definition of child abuse and neglect shapes the deliberation of the individual who must invoke state action.

The social worker knows that the criminal law rarely acts preventively, but that a dependency and neglect action may prevent the neglect of a baby's nutritional needs which, otherwise, might lead to death. The prosecutor must satisfy a standard of proof beyond a reasonable doubt because the purpose of criminal law is to punish and deter, sometimes by incarceration. The social worker's task is to assess the status of the child as endangered or not. Parental culpability, if present, is more often than not an irrelevant or distracting feature of the child protection proceeding brought by the social services department. A "no-fault" understanding may be much more helpful in protecting the child than entertaining ideas of culpability, with the focus on parental capacity to meet the minimal needs of a given child.

Adjudication of Child Abuse and Neglect

Evidentiary considerations and the use of children as witnesses (see Part II, Chapters 2 & 3) are also important considerations as part of the process that decides whether or not a particular child is abused or neglected. As a judge, or jury in some states, considers whether the legal definition of child abuse or neglect is met, the facts of the case are presented by direct and indirect evidence. The opinions of both nonexperts and experts may be important, although what is directly observed and related affects judges and jurors most strongly. Most individuals prefer to draw their own conclusions, and facts that speak for themselves often carry more weight than even informed opinion.

Lay opinion is an essential feature of society's defining abuse and neglect. Ordinary citizens are manifesting their belief that a child is maltreated when they report a suspected case. Jurors represent community standards. Jurors clarify that it is not a legislature or executive, like the president or governor, which sets standards of minimal child care in the United States. Expert opinion may inform, and indeed may strongly affect, fact-finding by judges and jury, but community standards are the ultimate arbiter.

DIFFERENT TYPES OF ABUSE AND NEGLECT

By examining case law decisions and statutes on various types of abuse or neglect, a sense of what is tolerated in the care of children in the United States can be developed. For many survivors of physical abuse, sexual abuse and neglect, the emotional harm to the child can be more persistent and difficult to treat than physical problems.[7] As the various types of abuse and neglect are reviewed, the child advocate must remember that visible harm is a marker for many types of, if sometimes less obvious, emotional drainage. An incapacity to trust, disorders of empathy, poor impulse control, great confusion about one's self and a poor sense of what is right and wrong other than what expediency suggests are typical problems of abused and neglected children. The opportunity to provide protection and treatment for a child's needs, both clear and subtle, is the justification for studying either "the symptoms the child presents" or "the actions of caretaking adults."[8]

Physical Abuse

Some statutes list examples of harms which are actionable:

> skin bruising, bleeding, . . . burns, fracture of any bone, subdural hematoma, soft tissue swelling . . .[9]

In both criminal and civil settings, medical testimony about the injury may help the judge or jury understand that the injuries were not accidental[10] or that they occurred at different times. Since reasonable corporeal punishment may be an excuse for some physical abuse, testimony may need to be introduced to refute such a claim.[11]

Photographs, x-rays and similar evidence may be very important for communicating the nature of the injuries. Claims that a child is easily burned or accident prone can also be addressed by pediatric child abuse experts. Since more than one person may be present, tending to confuse the issue of whether a parent has acted reasonably, "failure to protect" arguments[12] and other evidentiary approaches, as discussed in Part II, Chapter 2 should be considered.

Sexual Abuse

The intent of the caretaker may be raised by the respondent as an explanation or excuse for sexual contact. This may be approached by looking at a reasonable standard (What would a reasonable person do?) or by a subjective standard (What did the victim feel or observe?). For example, a responsible person is unlikely to accept as standard parenting practice that genital or oral penetration of a child's genital or anal orifices is nonsexual, nonintrusive and entirely harmless without clear medical or basic care justifications.

Because clear physical findings are unusual in many sexual abuse cases, the presence or absence of sexual abuse is often defined by statements or behaviors of the child. For that reason, the child advocate should be familiar with diagnostic books, writing and practice in the field. A good brief example of the information needed is found in a booklet by David P. H. Jones and Mary McQuiston entitled *Interviewing the Sexually Abused Child*.[13]

In reviewing the definition of sexual abuse for epidemiological purposes, Finkelhor and Hotaling[14] included acts involving penile penetration of or by the child; molestation with genital contact; inappropriate hugging, kissing or fondling of breasts, buttocks or other nongenital areas; stimulating penile or vaginal fondling of or by the child and permitting prostitution, commercial pornography, sexual acts in the presence of the caretaker or permitting sexual exploitation by others. While criminal statutes have explicit requirements, the broader provisions of dependency and neglect law arguably would encompass all of these behaviors. (For more information on determining sexual abuse, refer to Part II, Chapter 3.)

Neglect

Neglect is at least as pervasive as abuse and is especially salient to child development.[15] It can range from deadly to disabling in its effects on children. There are many varieties of deprivation, but because neglect is marked by the *absence* of needed care, it is difficult to define and to alter.

Poverty alone is not a sufficient basis for adjudicating neglect.[16] Failure to provide necessary food, shelter or clothing can, however, be evidence of generally improper parental care and custody.[17] Even with minimal income, most parents love and care for their children in at least adequate fashion, and some parents provide astonishing care in the face of the most stringent conditions. Other parents, even with support in the form of Aid to Families with Dependent Children, help in finding jobs or assistance with food and shelter by churches or other public agencies, do not meet their children's minimal needs. Love, affection, emotional consistency and support can be provided by the poorest parents, and courts seem universally to have recognized the distinction between economic and emotional impoverishment. Thus, frequent housing moves, school changes and job changes can be associated with poverty or with chaotic and impulse-ridden behavior independent of economic circumstances.

It is a practical task to understand the degree to which these problems are irreversibly internalized in the caretakers, and to such a degree that a child will, more or less, inevitably be emotionally deprived. One result of some parenting is that children are emotionally abandoned, an extreme form of denying love and affection with resultant effects on self-concept, capacity and achievement. Destruction of attachment in such cases may be as severe as parental death or physical abandonment, or worse, in the sense that adequate substitute care is blocked.

Medical Care Neglect

Table 1 summarizes the factors influencing courts in the United States to order medical care over parental objection.[18] In addition, the child advocate will consider the degree to which the age of the child and internalization of values is such that ordering intervention has the same negative impact that overriding the will of an adult might have. The child advocate will also want to consider whether the procedure is one that needs to take place only once, or if the procedure must be compulsively complied with over time. A mature minor or child under strong external compulsion to fight intervention for a chronic condition may create a situation in which more harm is caused by unavoidable, sudden cessation of the regimen than the harm that would have occurred had no procedure ever been ordered.

Prenatal Neglect

There are situations in which blood transfusions and Caesarean sections have been ordered on behalf of unborn children.[19] Table 2 summarizes the increasing levels of intrusion on the privacy rights of mothers which might be justified by unusually compelling factual situations.[20]

CONCLUSION

The changing nature of the meaning of "neglect", our reliance in law on fact patterns in individual cases, the relationship between "minimal" and "reasonable" parenting, and the contràst between notions of parental culpability and the fundamental needs of children must all be considered in defining and responding to both child abuse and neglect. Effective child advocacy requires an understanding of the different roles that the definitions of abuse and neglect play,

Table 1.

Factors Likely to Determine Court Decisions in Cases of Medical Care Neglect in the United States

Factors Likely to Support Legal Intervention	Least Basis on Which *Most* But Not All Courts Would Order Intervention	Factors Likely to Deter Legal Orders
1. Full informed consent procedure is followed		2. Lack of medical data for parent or court
3. Severity: outcome of failure to treat is death	Severity: outcome of failure to treat is blindness, deafness, paralysis, retardation, or other severe physical or mental impairment	4. Outcome is disfigurement, psychological harm or marginally handicapping or impairing condition (but at least one court has ordered intervention for "cosmetic" surgery and another for dental caries and fractured teeth)
5. Delay increases probability of harm	Effect of delay is uncertain	6. Decision can wait for child's emancipation
7. Treatment or intervention is well-established, universally accepted by medical profession		8. Treatment is experimental, untested or contested by at least some within the medical profession
9. Probability of success is very high (e.g., 75–85% or higher)	Probability of success at least 50%	10. Probability of success less than 50%
11. Negative consequences or contraindications are minimal in severity		12. Consequences include severe pain, impairment, or similar result
13. Negative consequences or contraindications are unlikely		14. Negative consequences certain
15. Child will have "high quality," full life-span or "normal" life in other respects	Child will not be greatly handicapped in other respects (i.e., not "right-to-die" possibility)	16. Child severely handicapped in ways not affected by treatment, or otherwise in "right-to-die" condition
17. Older child consents to treatment		18. Older child objects to treatment
19. No alternative will provide better, more probable benefit		20. Reasonable alternatives exist

---

Table 2.
Legal and Practical Alternatives for the Protection of the Unborn

The alternatives which should be examined in prenatal neglect cases include the following. The alternatives represent increasingly intrusive steps and therefore require an increasingly strong medical, social, or psychiatric basis. All of these steps assume that adequate attempts at voluntary compliance have been undertaken.

1. Document prenatal behavior harmful to the child as a method of establishing a syndrome or pattern of conduct justifying immediate court action as soon as the child is born.
2. Ask the court to take jurisdiction over the unborn child, and to appoint a guardian ad litem for the unborn child.
3. Ask the court to order a social investigation of the family.
4. Ask the court to order a medical or psychiatric examination of the mother (or father).
5. Ask the court to order a medical regimen, following the application of informed consent principles and considering primarily procedures benign or beneficial to the mother.
6. Ask the court to order fetal monitoring or other intervention, such as court-ordered Caesarean section, if and only if, relatively benign to the mother.
7. The most restrictive alternative possible is an order of confinement. Involuntary confinement or restriction of physical activities creates special problems of right to travel, and special concerns of due process under law. While such a step could occur only under the most extraordinary of circumstances, involuntary evaluation and treatments do occur rather frequently in mental health cases and cannot be ruled out in some prenatal abuse cases.

---

and understanding how to obtain the various types of knowledge necessary to assure that, in working towards better, stronger and more self-fulfilled citizens in a democracy, the lowest common denominator for childhood is not patently an abusive or neglectful standard of care.

FOOTNOTES

1. M. G. Paulsen, "Child Abuse Reporting Laws: The Shape of the Legislation," *Columbia Law Review* 67:1, 1967; M. G. Paulsen, "The Legal Framework for Child Protection," *Columbia Law Review* 66:679, 1966.

2. Douglas J. Besharov, "The Legal Aspects of Reporting Known and Suspected Child Abuse and Neglect," *Villanova University Law Review* 23:458, 1978.

3. Department of Health, Education and Welfare (DHEW), "Model Child Protection Act with Commentary" (Draft), August 1977.

4. Id.

5. Department of Health and Human Services (DHHS), "State Statutes Related to Child Abuse and Neglect: 1984," Vol. 1 (Complete Version in State Order), June 1985.

6. *Florida v. Groff,* 409 So.2d 44, (Fla. App. 1981).

7. Harold P. Martin, *The Abused Child: A Multidisciplinary Approach to Developmental Issues and Treatment,* Ballinger Publishing Company, Cambridge, MA.: 1976.

8. Ruth S. Kempe and C. Henry Kempe, *Child Abuse,* Fontana/Open Books, London: 1978.

9. *Colorado Revised Statutes,* Section 19-10-103(1) (1978).

10. *United States v. Woods,* 484 F.2d 127 (4th Circuit 1973); *United States v. Grady,* 481 F.2d 1106 (DC Circuit 1973).

11. *People v. Henson,* 304 N.E.2d 358 (NY 1973); *People v. Hoehl,* 568 P.2d 484 (Colo. 1977).

12. *People v. Strohm,* 523 P.2d 973 (Colo. 1974).

13. David P. H. Jones and Mary McQuiston, *Interviewing the Sexually Abused Child,* C. Henry Kempe National Center, Denver, CO.: 1985.

14. D. Finkelhor and G. T. Hotaling, "Sexual Abuse in the National Incidence Study of Child Abuse and Neglect: An Appraisal," *Child Abuse and Neglect* 8:23, 1984.

15. R. K. Oates, "Similarities and Differences Between Nonorganic Failure-to-Thrive and Deprivation Dwarfism," *Child Abuse and Neglect* 8:439, 1984.

16. *State ex rel Johnson,* 175 P.2d 486 (Utah 1946); *In re Fisher,* 545 P.2d 654 (Mont. 1976); *In re Raya,* 63 Cal. Rptr. 252 (App. 1967).

17. *In re Loomis,* 195 Neb. 552, 239 N.W.2d 266 (1976).

18. Donald C. Bross, "Medical Care Neglect", *Child Abuse and Neglect* 6:375, 1982.

19. Donald C. Bross and A. Meredyth, "Neglect of the Unborn Child: An Analysis Based on Law in the United States," *Child Abuse and Neglect* 3:643, 1979.

20. Id.

——— PART II ———

Issues for the Child's Representative

AN INTRODUCTION
TO CHILD REPRESENTATION

Donald C. Bross, J.D., Ph.D.

Representation of one person by another has been a traditional focus of law. This tradition holds that representation is a skill to be learned and practiced, defined by standards and subject to review and regulation. Effective representation of children by lawyers or nonlawyers demands care and understanding that can be guided by relevant legal tradition and principle. Since the type of representation described here developed from representation of maltreated children, and since the working assumption is that representation can be beneficial, some points supporting the assumption of potential benefit should be made.

There is at least some experience to indicate that effective representation of incompetents can decrease questionable, involuntary mental health intervention,[1] and, in the example of children specifically, increase family compliance with treatment plans,[2] decrease time in foster care[3] and increase chances for freeing children for adoption when adoption is strongly indicated.[4]

ARGUMENTS FOR AND AGAINST
REPRESENTATION OF CHILDREN

Against a background of representation of adult interests so prevalent that many express concern as to the excessive numbers of lawyers and laws in the United States, many objections to independent child representation can, nevertheless, be raised. For example, it can be argued that the positions of the parent and the intervening agency will also be a good representation of the child's needs: no additional information about the child or on behalf of the child will be necessary before the judge decides a case. However, the very reason the child's case appears in court is that the judgment of the parents is in question. Also, many considerations of budget, policy and personality determine the representation of protective services agencies. Independence in representation is, by definition, different than joint representation.

The notion of independent representation of children by lawyers has been challenged as nonsensical on the basis that without a client competent to negotiate, direct and monitor the service, a meaningful client–professional relationship cannot exist. For hundreds of years, on the other hand, lawyers have been appointed to represent and safeguard the interests of incompetents. Representation of the person or the property of incompetents, whether these individuals are seen as "clients" or not, is expressed in terms such as conservator, guardian and guardian *ad litem.* It is no longer a question that objective standards can be established for representation of incompetent adults or other individuals. In addition, most children fairly quickly grow old enough to express wishes, needs or interests that should be considered and weighed by any representative of a client. If a child directs the representative to argue against what the reasonable advocate might construe as the best interest of the child, the advocate can recognize the conflict, alert the court and, if appropriate, work to see that the minor's directives, and his or her reasonable "best interests," are both independently well-presented, perhaps by separate advocates.

The presence of a child's independent representative at the legal proceedings may influence the outcome. This is the purpose of representation. If the influences of the child's representative affect the outcome of a hearing adversely from the perspective of parents or a protective services agency, the party which does not prevail may consider the presence of the child representative unfair. It is traditional in law, however, to allow interest which may diverge during a proceeding to be separately advocated, even if the complexity results in the appointment of many different advocates. The liaisons that occur are presumed to be fair, no matter what the outcome, if all are assured that the representative is independent and competent.

Many judges remain reluctant to have children independently represented in cases where children's interests visibly or potentially will conflict with others in court. If the judge becomes aware that other data need to be presented, it is argued; then additional hearings or testimony can be ordered. Practically, there may be no manifest reason to order an investigation, further development of evidence or appointment of counsel because the basis for such a decision is often in the control of parties not responsive to a child's minimal needs. Judges do not have time to seek out alternative sources of evidence or alternative dispositions. Finally, if the judge is to avoid subverting the court's role of neutral fact-finding and decision-making, the judge cannot act with primary responsibility for the independent representation of the child. Accountability is a major concern in the representation of incompetents, and the court has the primary responsibility of monitoring and responding to questions about the quality of such representation.[5]

KNOWLEDGE FOR THE JOB

Brian Fraser has provided the best framework for independent representation of the abused or neglected child in a classic law review article which should be available to every person representing maltreated children.[6] In fulfilling the role of representing the child, Fraser writes

> The guardian *ad litem* assumes four functions . . . :
>
> ■ An *investigator* whose task is to ferret out all of the relevant facts;
> ■ An *advocate* whose task is to insure that all the relevant facts are before the court at all hearings;
> ■ A *counsel* whose task it is to insure that the court has before it at the dispositional hearing all available options; and
> ■ A *guardian* in the simplest sense of the word, whose task it is to insure that the child's interests are fully protected.[7]

Because children are different at different ages, as well as being individually unique, the child's representative will find it extremely difficult to fulfill these tasks without the constant availability of individuals who work with children routinely, preferably with a number of different types of training. Child developmental specialists, adolescent specialists, pediatricians, child and adult psychologists and psychiatrists, and clinical social workers are among those individuals who can support and challenge the person attempting to represent the child's best interests. Without personal knowledge or available consultants in these areas, the child's representative must be concerned that harm may be done in the name of doing good. While these sources of knowledge alone will not assure success, they decrease the chances for rash, erroneous or futile responses and increase the prospects for thoughtful and informed decisions. Sources of these types of expertise are discussed below.

Many types of law may apply to the situation of an abused or neglected child. The lawyer representative must be prepared to apply principles, statutes and cases from dependency and neglect, mental health, tort, administrative law, criminal law, probate and conservatorship, health law, tax law, domestic relations and constitutional law among many special legal areas. The nonlawyer representative must have access to an individual child's needs, and know enough to be aware when a particular approach or issue has not been identified and should be.

STAGES OF LEGAL INTERVENTION

Lawyers are familiar with the process of filing an action, discovery, pretrial conferences, adjudication and disposition. Representatives of children must understand the significance of each of these stages and be involved appropriately.

Reporting, Filing a Court Action and Other Preliminary Matters

Most cases of child abuse and neglect in the United States now come to attention because of mandatory reporting laws. These laws provide specific requirements for reporting, and some also establish important policies related to waiver of confidentiality and privilege, access to medical and other information, definitions and interagency cooperation. While reporting statutes usually set forth the required agency response, the expected response may not occur. In particular, if a case is not pursued when knowledgeable individuals strongly believe there is a basis to proceed and that further investigation is essential, many states have procedures for bringing possible child abuse and neglect into court without the immediate cooperation of child protection services. Until a cause of action is filed on behalf of a child, most of the protections of law may be unavailable, i.e., unenforceable. On the other hand, there may be no basis for intervention, no adequate basis or a voluntary agreement between the caretakers and the protective services agency may be deemed sufficient. In these latter situations, it is unlikely that a representative of the child will be appointed—a policy that sometimes should be re-examined.

Evaluation and Discovery

Once a representative is appointed, there are a number of immediate issues to be addressed, including the safety and condition of the child, other legal matters pending and the current physical and legal custody of the child. The initial placement of a child in custody may be the most important decision in a case. A necessary placement in a good foster home may create a long-term place of safety. An unnecessary placement may well harm a child more than it helps, as may a placement in a foster setting that does not meet the child's needs. Foster placements routinely last longer than anticipated. The importance of custody hearings is considerable, and is covered separately below and elsewhere in this book.

When developmental information, medical information about the child or the mental status of parental caretakers may help determine the child's safety, court-ordered evaluations should be sought before trial. Other information that might be sought through pretrial discovery orders, once other means have failed, includes prior reports or findings of abuse or neglect, physical evidence from the house, photographs of the child, x-rays, tests on bodily fluids, bite mark impressions, hair samples and other kinds of forensic evidence. Discovery is commonly used in law, even used to excess in some lawsuits. In children's cases, the expense, and lack of common implementation of discovery principles in protective services actions, will often raise barriers to the child representative's appropriate use of pretrial discovery. Good trial preparation requires persistence and innovation in children's law.

Pretrial and Negotiation

Many judges use the standard legal approach of a pretrial meeting or hearing to focus the prospective adjudicatory hearing on just those factual and legal issues which must be addressed in trial, and which cannot be stipulated to or agreed to prior to trial. This opportunity can reduce the costs of litigation, the time which must pass before the outcome of the case is clear, and may lead to proposals for an out-of-court settlement.

The child's representative must be very clear as to what is being negotiated in the "informal adjustment," out-of-court settlement, stipulation or similar agreement. At least one study suggests that court-ordered treatment of abusive situations is more likely to be completed than voluntary agreements,[8] notwithstanding traditional thinking that mental health treatment is probably most beneficial for the person who recognizes that there is a problem. Without an admission on the record, formally accepted by the court, it is very easy for a parental custodian to revert to earlier disclaimers to the fact that the child has not been well-enough cared for, or that the child has been injured because of unacceptable actions or neglect by the parent.

What must not be negotiated away is long-term, court-monitored safety for a child who has been subjected to provable and unacceptable abuse or neglect. It is very easy to be optimistic about a family situation early, since all wish the best for the child and parent involved, but much better to be able to be optimistic late in the case.

Adjudication

Without a lawyer representing the child at trial, the child is inevitably at a disadvantage. Some issues, of course, involve both legal and nonlegal judgments. For example, the child's representative must be able to factor in the effects of having or not having the child present at hearings. The effects on the child, as well as the impact on the judge or jury, should be weighed. Other issues are more likely to be part of classic legal training and skills, i.e., being well-prepared on the specific factual and legal issues to be tried.

The results of child abuse and neglect trials depend on the evidence presented, including testimony, as well as the arguments made. The child representative must be aware that in many cases involving children, the preparation of lay and expert witnesses is totally inadequate. Proper preparation includes care in choosing witnesses, feeling assured that they understand the essential factual and legal issues in the case and knowing that they understand the rights and limitations of their roles as witnesses. This includes work in advance of the case to answer questions and reassure witnesses so that they will be more comfortable with the court process and their own performances.

Preparation for trial highlights the importance of expert witnesses for testimony. The value of an expert witness in child abuse and neglect is usually correlated closely with her or his ability to diagnose and treat children or adults within a framework of child care.

In assessing the choice of evaluation and treatment experts, the child's advocate realizes that many individuals have titles or degrees which suggest competency with respect to child abuse and neglect when, in fact, neither training nor experience gives them reliable insight. Individuals with enough actual experience in evaluating children and parents to have learned from their errors, individuals with the capacity and sensitivity to separate clearly the needs of children and parents, and individuals with a solid commitment to the importance of childhood should be preferred.

Disposition

Some of the many factors that may need to be examined in a dispositional hearing are listed in Part III. The availability of dispositional alternatives, however, is often determined by what happened in the investigation, pretrial preparation and negotiations, and the nature of the adjudication. In many jurisdictions, it is not routine to recognize from the beginning that termination of the parent–child legal relationship is a possible outcome. Notice of this possibility to parental caretakers and full awareness of the seriousness of these proceedings should be obtained early in the case. Absent fathers, putative fathers or mothers who have rarely been involved in the care of a child should, nevertheless, be served and brought into a case early to prevent later questions as to the fairness and completeness of the legal proceedings. It is unfortunately common that such issues wait until a child is made available for adoption before the obstacle of failure to serve all parties is recognized.

At disposition the adequacy of early placement efforts is often put to the test. If the placement was good, the best for the child will probably be obvious, and very well may be with the original placement family. The original placement family may be the original biological family or a foster family. If the original placement was broken or is not suitable for long-term care, then the options are often all likely to be less attractive.

Termination of the parent–child relationship is an important option when a child has no reasonable prospects for growing up in his or her original family. Rather than approaching termination as a "fault issue," in which freeing the child for adoption is seen as justified by the aggravated nature of parental conduct, a "no-fault" approach is often better for the child advocate. This approach recognizes that in most cases it is not the fault of parents that they cannot provide the minimally adequate care that a given child needs. It also permits all involved in the case to recognize that not every birth parent and birth child are a fit for each other, and that mutually irreconcilable differences can exist between any two humans. Finally, the no-fault understanding of the situation may allow treating professionals to feel less like failures when no currently available therapy offers any reasonable prospects for improving the parenting capacity of the individuals involved.

It is likely that no one except the child representative will focus on the child's need for therapy. Most children who have been abused have special needs that must be addressed, or there will be little chance for a successful long-term parent–child relationship between abused and abuser. Since children continue to grow and develop special relationships with whomever is providing primary care, the child advocate must take a "time is of the essence" approach to dispositional plans and review. It is in the interest of a child to be with a biological parent who can do at least reasonably well, since there is no clear evidence as to what standards would reflect reasonable parenting. On the other hand, the child's representative cannot stand by while too much experimentation takes place, particularly with the life of a young child. The youngest children especially cannot wait and stop growing up while repeated attempts are made for minimal adequacy in care. Related to the issue of minimal adequacy in care is concern for the monitoring of a child in foster care and an awareness of favorable or unfavorable changes during a placement.

CUSTODY HEARINGS

Custody hearings typically can occur at any time from the beginning of a child protection process to the end. The implication of custody hearings at different stages in the protection process is superficially similar; that is, the decision about who will have immediate care of the child is always at issue. The underlying issues of different custody hearings, however, can shift drastically. For example, temporary custody hearings are more likely to occur early in a case, and focus on the immediate safety of the child. Less often recognized, is the idea that temporary custody may have a diagnostic focus. By the dispositional phase, hearings may be concerned not only with the child's immediate safety and minimal care, but also long-term custody, permanency and termination of the parent–child legal relationship. Each hearing, of course, may have any of these elements as an issue to a greater or lesser degree.

Protective Custody

The information available to a protective services agency and the court when a child is first evaluated for abuse or neglect is likely to be limited. All of the data needed for custody hearings can almost never be obtained in the first custody hearing, unless a case has already been opened and closed in the past. (See Part III, Chapter 2.) The child's representative will be aware that the younger a child, the greater the worry if life threatening conditions exist in the child's home of origin. At the same time, the impact of separation and loss on the younger child must also be a concern. If the safety of a child who has been injured or seriously deprived cannot be clearly guaranteed, then the child's representative will want to focus on seeing that the foster placement is adequate, that the data needed to establish the safety or danger will be promptly forthcoming, and that the effects of separation will be minimized. Knowledge of child development and access to experienced, independent child care specialists is essential in these matters. While most temporary custody hearings are held around the theme of protection, temporary custody may also be an aid to, or even necessary for, diagnosis.

Diagnostic Custody

There is relatively little specific case law on temporary custody for the purpose of evaluation, but the issue is fairly common and important. The lack of appellate law is, in part, due to the timing of diagnostic custody, usually early in the case before there is a final court ruling to appeal. The use of temporary custody for diagnostic or evaluative purposes also frequently occurs with some basis for arguing that the child is in imminent danger and in need of protective custody. A child who has suffered nonaccidental trauma, reportedly because the child is clumsy or accident-prone, may need to be placed to prevent similar, avoidable injuries in the future. The same placement should help establish that a minimally safe environment will prevent such injuries, whatever the child's "fault" or contribution to the injuries or condition. Too often, children are blamed for being clumsy, accident-prone, provocative or seductive with the bare allegation taken as an established fact.

More subtly, but gravely important, is the fact that a suspected diagnosis of nonorganic failure-to-thrive or Munchausen's Syndrome by Proxy[9] may be confirmable only if the child is placed in a different environment and carefully nurtured and monitored. In order to make a diagnosis by exclusion of this nature, temporary custody should be seen as part of the pretrial discovery process in a legal sense, as well as an occasionally necessary procedure for medical diagnosis. Since each of these neglect conditions can be fatal, careful attention to making separation as nontraumatic as possible through transition objects and other techniques eases the burden of making these types of placement recommendations.

Notably, if a child who should show separation anxiety and other signs of loss, does so minimally or not at all, most child development experts would be concerned about the nature of the parent–child attachment. Careful monitoring and support of the child can make the separation diagnosis with minimal trauma, or may reveal a relationship so aversive that only improvement in the child's condition results.

Long-Term Placement[10]

Notwithstanding reasonable efforts to reduce the use of foster care, some children will be placed, and the challenge is to increase the prospects that less harm or even some therapeutic value will result. Current federal legislation conditions some state funding on compliance with requirements of judicial review of placement changes, foster care standards and other permanency planning reforms.[11] The child's representative must be fully aware of the risk to children of foster care, especially when changes in foster care occur. In addition to the risks of separation, psychological loss and attachment disorders,[12] children in foster care may suffer physical[13] and sexual[14] abuse. Mistakes for the child's representative include not learning from the foster care parents and not probing the reasons for choices of a given foster home and changes in the foster placement. The match between a child with special problems and a foster or adoptive family is often problematic. On the other hand, it would also be a mistake not to recognize that foster parents, like biological parents, may need special support as they try to deal with a specific child.

Perhaps the greatest error is to fail to consider before a foster placement whether it is a placement of sufficient quality that the foster parents might eventually be eligible to adopt. Since foster care can become long-term, despite the best efforts to hasten termination or a return home, it is possible to relax at least a little if there is some feeling that the attachments that typically can develop between a child and foster parents are beneficial to the child for the long term.

To not even consider the possibility of termination in the beginning of a child abuse or neglect case may be cause for later regret. It is best to be clear about what is needed from the beginning and to lay the groundwork for a permanent home early. A clear understanding of what is minimally needed for a child stated early will give biological parents their best chance of knowing how to respond, and assure that neither rising expectations of the parents nor evasions related to a lack of notice will block a fair and prompt decision with respect to the child's long-term placement.

There are many obstacles to termination, not the least of which are the associated feelings of failure commonly expressed by treatment and legal professionals alike. The child's representative will perceive that, in some cases, it is no one's fault that a parent and child are irreconcilably incompatible, and that making the child a victim of this incompatibility cannot be justified even by an argument that the child is all the parent has. From a child's perspective, it is not necessarily the severity of the injury or neglect, but rather the prospect that less than minimal care will continue. The doctrines of waiver, estoppel or laches may be applied to reduce the time that children wait for needed secure placement.

PERSONAL ISSUES FOR THE CHILD REPRESENTATIVE

Because most children cannot hold the advocate responsible for inadequate representation, issues of self-regulation by the child advocate are important. Some of these issues are discussed at the end of Chapter 6, Professional and Agency Liability. Understanding what one expects for and of the children, parents and professionals will help the child representative avoid overreaching, and to focus advocacy on the essential questions. It is all too easy to rationalize that the money paid is not sufficient for the time required, or that no one will realize if not all that is possible is being done.

The need for specialized knowledge, the need for emotional support when mistakes are made or results are bad, and the need for accountability all militate against the solo approach to child advocacy. Over the long term, child representatives are more likely to provide consistently strong and effective representation when they are constantly supported, trained and monitored by colleagues who have different backgrounds, but share the same goals.

———————

FOOTNOTES

1. "When a Man Needs a Lawyer," *Transaction* (1969), cited in J. Grossman and J. Ladinsky (eds.), *Law and Society Review* 5:431, 1971.

2. D. A. Wolfe, J. Aragona, K. Kaufman and J. Sandler, "The Importance of Adjudication in the Treatment of Child Abuse: Some Preliminary Findings," *Child Abuse and Neglect* 4:127, 1980.

3. S. Browne and J. D. Carr, *GAL Project Evaluation,* Denver, CO.: 1984.

4. D. H. Schetky, R. Angell, C. V. Morrison and W. H. Sack, "Parents Who Fail: A Study of 51 Cases of Termination of Parental Rights," *Journal of the American Academy of Child Psychiatry* 18:366, 1979.

5. *Seaton v. Tohill,* 11 Colo. App. 211, 53 P. 170 (1898).

6. B. S. Fraser, "Independent Representation for the Abused and Neglected Child: The Guardian ad Litem," *California Western Law Review* 13:16, 1976.

7. Id.

8. See D. A. Wolfe, et al, *supra* note 2.

9. *United States v. Woods,* 484 F.2d 127 (4th Cir 1973).

10. Excerpted in part from Donald C. Bross, "Practical Child Advocacy: Lessons from Selected Cases," in *Practical Child Advocacy,* Ann M. Haralambie (ed.), National Association of Counsel for Children, Tucson, AZ.: 1982.

11. The Adoption Assistance and Child Welfare Act of 1980, P.L. 96–272. See especially 42 USC Section 671 et seq.

12. Joseph Goldstein, Anna Freud and Albert J. Solnit, *Beyond the Best Interests of the Child,* Free Press, New York: 1973.

13. *Koepf v. York,* 198 Neb. 67, 251 N.W.2d 866 (1977).

14. *Doe v. New York City Dept. of Soc. Serv.* 649 F.2d 134 (2d Cir 1981).

EVIDENTIARY ISSUES IN CASES INVOLVING CHILDREN

Laura Freeman Michaels, Esq.

Many evidentiary considerations arise for child advocates when preparing for legal proceedings. Lawyers need to develop a repertoire of tactics and strategies to prove their cases. Nonlawyers involved in the legal system should also have an appreciation for basic evidence law so that they can most effectively assist in investigating, preparing, and providing testimony and other forms of evidence in cases concerning the protection of children.

The federal rules of evidence are emphasized here since they are in effect in the federal system and in more than half of the states. In addition, they act as a model to other states which have not adopted them in their entirety. Specific rules and their applications will vary depending on whether the proceeding is civil or criminal, and according to individual state case law and statutes. In this chapter, evidentiary issues are set forth in the form of a general foundation for practitioners to use in fashioning specific approaches in their work on behalf of children in actual cases.

SUFFICIENCY OF EVIDENCE

Standards of Proof

The probative value of a statement or physical finding often cannot be determined on its face. It may be merely a part of a large array of evidentiary bits and pieces, or it may be the only indication of mistreatment of a child. A thorough investigation at the early stages of a case is crucial to the advocate's full understanding and subsequent effective representation of the child client.

The type of hearing will also determine the strength of the evidence uncovered. What may be sufficient to justify intervention in the lives of family members may not be sufficient to imprison the perpetrator. Therefore, the distinction between the civil and criminal settings is important. Criminal prosecution of child abuse cases is still rare compared to the large number of cases in the dependency and neglect process. A major reason for this is that the prosecutors who have the discretion to charge a perpetrator with a crime frequently find that in their estimations there is insufficient evidence to file a criminal action. However, even with a small amount of evidence, an adjudication of dependency or neglect may be sustained. The authority of the civil court should not be underestimated for in it lies the power to assure safe placement, require treatment and, if necessary, to terminate parental rights.

The differing standards of proof of the various proceedings affect what will be considered to be sufficient evidence in a given case. The highest burden—beyond a reasonable doubt— is used in the criminal setting because a determination is being made as to the guilt or innocence of the adult perpetrator. The violation of a criminal statute is charged and the accused may be punished by the state if found guilty.

By contrast, the civil adjudication hearing does not judge guilt or innocence. It is rather a *determination of the status of the child.* An adjudication of dependency, abuse, neglect or other statutory requirement of a particular jurisdiction allows the state to intervene in the lives of the child and family members. Since the purpose of the proceeding is to enable intervention and not to punish, the standard of proof is usually the most lenient—preponderance of the evidence. Although some states have moved to the clear and convincing standard for adjudications, preponderance of the evidence is the better rule from the point of view of the child victim because of the difficulties of proof and the child's vulnerability to further harm.

In a termination hearing, the intermediate burden—clear and convincing—is universally used as is required by the U.S. Supreme Court.[1] Since the parent–child relationship may be permanently severed, this higher burden must be met even in jurisdictions which use the preponderance standard in the adjudication stage.

The actual effect of the differing standards of proof may be more academic than practical. The degree of intervention sought in a case may influence the judge in determining what will be considered sufficient evidence.[2] Moreover, many judges who preside over juvenile civil proceedings do not require strict compliance with the rules of evidence. Hearsay often comes in unchallenged, and records are frequently admitted freely. However, since all judges are different and the general trend is toward stricter adherence to the rules, it is best to know the tools of evidence and how they are properly used.

Circumstantial Evidence

In the search for evidence, there is the troublesome possibility that little will surface. Admissions and eyewitnesses are rare. The child is often unwilling or unable to give a cogent account of the circumstances. In these cases where the truth is known only by the perpetrator, courts in several jurisdictions have adopted a *res ipsa loquitur* analogy for abuse cases.[3] Under this doctrine, evidence of injury to a child coupled with evidence of parental control at the time of the injury may create a presumption that the parent is responsible for the injury.

A New York court judge used this approach to make a finding of abuse in the case of a badly battered infant.

> Although the proof fails to point with certainty to one or both parents as the perpetrators of the abuse, the doctrine of *res ipsa loquitur* applies—the condition of the child speaks for itself, thus permitting an inference of abuse to be drawn from proof of the child's age and condition, and that the latter is such as in the ordinary course of things does not happen if the parent who has the responsibility and control of an infant is protective and non-abusive.[4]

DISCOVERY

In a civil case, the child advocate should consult the appropriate rules of procedure to determine which discovery devices are available for particular proceedings. Oral and written depositions, interrogatories, requests for admission, production of documents or property and motions for physical or mental examinations may be excellent means for gathering information. The extra effort put into acquiring evidence in the initial stages of the case will work to the advantage of the attorney in negotiations or at trial.

RECORDS, REPORTS AND EVALUATIONS

Social services reports, police reports and hospital records are essential sources of information. The best records are those that are kept in a professional manner setting forth a chronological history of observed behavior, statements made and other relevant facts. The person who prepared the report will be subject to cross-examination when the report is put into the record. Through the business record exception to the hearsay rule, the report or record may substitute for the live witness or witnesses, but cannot do more than a testifying witness could do if present.[5] Therefore, any hearsay statements in the record may be stricken unless another hearsay exception, other than the business record exception, can be shown to be applicable.[6]

Psychiatric or psychological evaluations of the parents or children may be ordered by the civil court or conducted by the agency as part of its investigation of the case. Evaluations made prior to adjudication may provide vital information as to the medical or developmental status of a child or the psychiatric status of a parent. They are also useful and sometimes indispensable to professionals when making placement and treatment decisions.

All states now have laws requiring that certain professionals report suspected cases of abuse and neglect. Although there appears to be a consensus that these laws are needed to protect children, the statutes in many jurisdictions are inconsistent and confusing. There is a need for clear legislation in this area to avoid leaving the professional uncertain about what must be reported, what may be reported and what must not be revealed.[7] The most appropriate practice for a professional is never to guarantee confidentiality with respect to communications regarding child abuse or neglect.

DEMONSTRATIVE EVIDENCE

Photographs are valuable pieces of evidence since they preserve and vividly show the condition of a child at the time of an injury. The defendant in a criminal case may try to argue that a given picture is inflammatory and will cause the jury to respond emotionally rather than rationally. On the other side, the state or child advocate may contend that the picture is necessary to accurately depict the nature and extent of the injury or cause of death. The determination is within the judge's discretion and normally pictures will be admitted. The test used is whether the probative value outweighs the prejudicial effect.[8] Enlargements are admissible according to the same test. To authenticate, any witness familiar with the scene depicted verifies that the photograph is an accurate representation.[9] Diagrams may also be admitted as an aid to the jury.[10]

For x-rays, the process for authentication is stricter since they depict conditions not visible to the ordinary senses. To lay a proper foundation, the x-ray should be identified as that of the child in issue and of the physical condition at the time in issue. Also, it should be shown that the x-ray was taken with a dependable, working instrument by a qualified person in an accurate manner.[11]

Other physical evidence such as clothes, blood samples, writings or weapons may be especially persuasive either as direct or circumstantial evidence of an abusive act. Such evidence may be admitted on the basis of testimony if it is a readily identifiable item, or by showing chain of custody in the instance of evidence susceptible to tampering or confusion.[12] Again, it is within the court's discretion to determine whether the probative value sufficiently outweighs the prejudicial effect.[13]

In criminal cases, defendants may be forced to give non-testimonial evidence for use against them at trial. This may include fingerprints or samples of handwriting, blood, hair, urine, saliva, bite mark impressions, or a voice exemplar. The fifth amendment of the Constitution only protects against compelled testimony.[14]

TESTIMONY

Experts

One of the most obvious and yet most neglected means of improving the quality of expert testimony is by pretrial preparation. The attorney should discuss likely questions and courtroom procedure with the prospective witness before the trial date. This is particularly true in the case of an expert inexperienced in giving courtroom testimony.

In court, the qualification of the witness as an expert is the first step in establishing credibility. It may be helpful to narrow the field of expertise to give more strength to the specific opinions given by the expert.[15] For example, a social worker who is part of a sexual abuse team may be qualified as an "expert in social work" or an "expert in sexual abuse." The latter description would give more credibility to an opinion regarding the dynamics of sexual abuse. The lawyer should keep in mind that expertise may be gained through time and experience, as well as from advanced educational degrees.

There are three forms of expert testimony. The first is testimony and opinion about facts within the personal knowledge of the expert. Second, is an opinion given by the expert on the basis of a hypothetical situation posed to her at trial. Third, the expert opinion may be based on evidence that is of the type reasonably relied on by experts in the particular field, but the expert does not have personal knowledge of the facts, nor has been provided with them in court.[16] An example of this is a diagnosis by a medical specialist ascertained by analyzing another doctor's report.

Treatises

Learned treatises may be used to rebut or impeach the opposing party's expert once the text is established as authoritative.[17] Under the federal rules, an attorney may use a learned treatise in support of her own witness.[18] As long as there is an expert (of either side) on the stand, the information from the text may come in for the truth of the matter asserted because of the learned treatise hearsay exception. The treatise itself does not go to the jury.

In 1961, Dr. C. Henry Kempe presented a paper to the American Medical Association which first identified the "battered child syndrome." Since the early 1970's, the diagnosis has been recognized by the courts as a proper subject for expert testimony.[19]

The classic definition of the syndrome was stated in *People v. Henson.*

> . . . the diagnosis is used in connection with very young children . . . and is based upon a finding that such a child exhibits evidence, among other injuries, of subdural hematoma, multiple fractures in various stages of healing, soft tissue swellings, or skin-bruising. Also pertinent to the diagnosis is evidence that the child is generally undernourished and that the severity and type of injury in evidence on his body is inconsistent with the parents' story of its occurrence . . . This sort of expert medical testimony—that the victim is a "battered child" coupled with additional proof, for instance, that the injuries occurred while the child was in the sole custody of the parents—would permit the jury to infer not only that the child's injuries were not accidental but that, in addition, they occurred at the culpable hands of its parents.[20]

Testimony regarding battered child syndrome or evidence of non-accidental trauma may be used to rebut claims of accident and to show a plan or scheme.[21]

Nonexperts

When gathering convincing testimony, the practitioner should be careful not to disregard the nonexpert. Often a relative, foster parent or neighbor may provide evidence that the experts have not seen or may have communicated too technically to the jury.[22] A neighbor may be able to give descriptions of the condition of a child based on ten years of observation rather than on a few evaluation sessions conducted specifically for the trial. A foster mother may be able to give concrete examples of a child's change in behavior following visits with the biological parents. Lay person opinions are admissible into evidence if they are based on the perception of the witness and are helpful to the trier of fact.[23]

Children's Testimony

In most jurisdictions, the common law disqualifications have been modified and there is no longer a specified minimum age of competency for a witness. Instead, it is determined on a case-by-case basis by the judge who considers the child's ability to perceive, remember, and communicate events, and to appreciate the duty to tell the truth.[24] Recent studies have shown that even young children can give reliable and valuable testimony.[25]

In an effort to protect the child witness from the trauma of courtroom testimony, several states have begun to develop procedures that permit the child victim to be questioned without directly confronting the perpetrator.[26] The use of videotaped depositions, closed circuit televisions and children's courtrooms, through which the child is insulated from the proceeding, raises constitutional considerations in a criminal case because defendants have the right to confront the witnesses against them.[27] The problem has not yet been clearly resolved by the U.S. Supreme Court. The leading case, *Ohio v. Roberts* sets out the general approach to these cases:

> . . . when a hearsay declarant is not present for cross-examination at trial, the Confrontation Clause normally requires a showing that he is unavailable. Even then his statement is admissible only if it bears adequate 'indicia of reliability'. Reliability can be inferred without more in a case where the evidence falls within a firmly rooted hearsay exception. In other cases, the evidence must be excluded, at least absent a showing of particularized guarantees of trustworthiness.[28]

Determining what should constitute sufficient unavailability and reliability has been the subject of articles by numerous scholars.[29] It is a delicate task to reconcile the need to protect the child witness with the right of a criminal defendant to confrontation by the accuser. Decisions on when and how to best present children's testimony are discussed in greater detail in the chapter "Protecting Child Witnesses."

Hearsay

Hearsay is defined as an out-of-court statement offered into evidence in order to prove the truth of the matter asserted in the statement.[30] When building a case and compiling the evidence, the practitioner may be faced with the common problem of getting out-of-court statements made by the child admitted into evidence. Finding an appropriate hearsay exception can enable the advocate to use a child's statement without putting the child on the stand. This approach may be necessary to protect the child from the trauma of testifying or it may be used when the child is unavailable to testify, either physically, mentally or emotionally.

There are several hearsay exceptions that may apply to cases involving children. Certain evidence may be admitted as nonassertive verbal or nonverbal conduct, avoiding the problem of hearsay altogether. For example, testimony about a child's behavior during play therapy would be admissible as the question of sincerity is averted when the child is not intending to communicate. Nonassertive conduct or statements may include precocious knowledge of sexual matters, anxiety in handling anatomical dolls or fear in the presence of a particular person.[31]

Probably the most often cited hearsay exception, especially in sexual abuse cases, is the excited utterance or spontaneous declaration. To use this exception, there must be a startling event, the statement must be said under the stress of the event, and the statement must concern the facts of the event.[32] In the case of a child's statement, a declaration may be considered to be spontaneous even when it is made hours after the precipitating event. This is because the child's sense of time is not completely developed and for a significant time following the event, he may still be under the stress of the nervous excitement.[33] A child's response to questioning may be found to be spontaneous.[34] Even statements made after viewing photographs as long as eight weeks after the actual event have been admitted under this exception.[35]

A statement may fall under the exception allowing into evidence a declaration of the speaker's "then existing mental, emotional or physical condition."[36] This could be used to admit a child's statement of pain or fear. *In Re Cheryl H.* admitted a three-year-old's statement to her therapist that her father molested her since it supplied "circumstantial evidence she had a certain state of mind, that is, a belief her father had hurt her and a dislike and fear of him based on that belief. Whether the statement is true or not is irrelevant to this use of the statement."[37]

Other admissible statements are those made for "purposes of medical diagnosis or treatment."[38] Under this exception, a child's declarations made to doctors or other medical personnel as to the general cause of the child's injury are admissible. With respect to statements identifying the perpetrator of the abuse, most jurisdictions have held that such declarations are beyond the scope of this rule and may not be admitted.[39] Some courts, however, have begun to challenge this assumption. The Wyoming Supreme Court extended the exception to admit a child's statement to a doctor as to who caused the injuries.[40] The court explained

> If our goal were simply to pursue common law tradition of stare decisis then the cited authorities must be recognized . . . In this instance however, the function of the court must be to pursue the transcendent goal of addressing the most pernicious social ailment which afflicts our society, family abuse, and more specifically, child abuse.[41]

The Michigan Court of Appeals allowed a doctor's testimony as to the perpetrator's identity holding that the child's revelation that her vaginal pain was caused by her father was "reasonably necessary to obtain relief."[42]

Some jurisdictions have applied the "complaint of rape" exception in sexual abuse cases. Under this theory, evidence of the complaint is considered a hearsay exception and the statement is admitted without the testimony of the victim.[43]

Many states have taken steps to expand the available hearsay exceptions with regard to statements that have a high probability of reliability. These new statutes give the practitioner a greater opportunity for getting out-of-court statements admitted. At least ten states have special hearsay exceptions for a child's statement of sexual abuse.[44] The language of the statutes vary from state to state, but all recognize the general trustworthiness of these statements. In addition, the federal rules include the "residual" hearsay exception.[45] There is a growing trend among the states to adopt this catchall exception.[46] It allows a statement to be admitted which does not fall under one of the enumerated exceptions, but is shown to have "equivalent guarantees of trustworthiness."[47]

Admissions may be offered into evidence as nonhearsay statements.[48] Adoptive admissions may also be acceptable. A statement by a mother's boyfriend that he was "high" when he burned her baby was held to be an adoptive admission by the mother since she was present when the statement was made and did not refute it.[49]

PRIOR ACTS

In a criminal case, evidence of other crimes or misconduct committed by the defendant is not admissible as evidence of the defendant's character or disposition to commit crimes.[50] Such evidence, however, may be admissible to show other issues such as motive,[51] intent,[52] absence of mistake or accident,[53] identity[54] or modus operandi.[55] When a child's injuries or cause of death is the result of an accumulation of injuries inflicted over a period of time, evidence of the several acts is directly relevant to prove the crime itself and, therefore, would not have to fit into one of the above extraneous evidence categories.[58]

In dependency and neglect cases, evidence of prior abusive acts to a child or even the child's siblings may be used in making the statutory adjudication and terminating the parent–child legal relationship.[57]

CONCLUSION

When children are clients, they must depend on their representatives to be responsive and competent. Unfortunately, overwhelmed attorneys often fail to extend sufficient effort in cases involving children due to lack of time, remuneration or accountability. Many valuable evidentiary tools and techniques are overlooked or ignored as too time consuming or expensive. In these critical life-determining situations, maximizing traditional as well as innovative approaches to investigating and proving cases should be a priority for the attorney. Through a combination of preparation and ingenuity, the advocate can more successfully provide representation that improves the quality of life for the child.

FOOTNOTES

1. *Santosky v. Kramer,* 455 U.S. 745 (1982).
2. Dept. of Health and Human Services. Pub. No. (OHDS) 80 -30268, *Child Abuse and Neglect Legislation: A Manual for Judges,* March 1981, p. 82.
3. *State v. Loss,* 295 Minn. 171, 204 N.W. 2d 404 (1973); *In re Tashyne L.,* 53 A.D.2d 629, 384 N.Y.S.2d 472 (1976); *In re S.,* 66 Misc.2d 683, 322 N.Y.S.2d 170 (Fam. Ct. 1971); *Higgins v. Dallas County Child Welfare Unit,* 544 S.W.2d 745 (Tex. Civ. App.—Dallas 1976).
4. *In re S., supra* note 3 at 181-2.

5. Fed. R. Evid. 803(6); *McCormick on Evidence,* Section 310 (3rd ed.) West Publishing Co., Minnesota: 1984.

6. See *infra* notes 30–48 and accompanying text.

7. See R. Weisberg and M. Wald, "Confidentiality Laws and State Efforts to Protect Abused or Neglected Children: The Need for Statutory Reform," *Family Law Quarterly* 18:143, 1984.

8. McCormick, *supra* section 212.

9. McCormick, *supra* section 214.

10. *State v. Prestridge,* 399 So.2d 564 (La. 1981).

11. 3 Wigmore: *Evidence.* Section 795 (Chadbourn rev. 1970).

12. McCormick, *supra* section 212.

13. Id.

14. U.S. Constitution, Amendment V.

15. Jon L. Lawritson, "Trial Issues in a Dependency and Neglect Proceeding," in *Advocacy for the Legal Interests of Children,* Donald C. Bross (ed.), National Association of Counsel for Children, Denver, CO.: 1980, p. 356.

16. Fed. R. Evid. 703.

17. Fed. R. Evid. 803(18).

18. Id.

19. *People v. Ewing,* 72 Cal. App.3d 714, 140 Cal. Rptr. 299 (1977); *People v. Jackson,* 18 Cal. App.3d 504, 95 Cal. Rptr. 919 (1971); *Comm. v. Labbe,* 373 N.E.2d 227 (Mass. App. 1978); *State v. Loss,* 295 Minn. 171, 204 N.W.2d 404 (1973); *People v. Henson* 33 N.Y.2d 63, 304 N.E.2d 358 (1973); *State v. Wilkerson* 295 N.C. 559, 247 S.E.2d 905 (1978).

20. *People v. Henson, supra* at 364.

21. See *infra* notes 50-56 and accompanying text.

22. Jon L. Lawritson, *supra* note 15, at 357.

23. Fed. R. Evid. 701.

24. McCormick, *supra* section 62.

25. See Gail Goodman, "The Accuracies and Inaccuracies of Children's Eyewitness Reports," in *Multidisciplinary Advocacy for Children,* Donald C. Bross (ed.), National Association of Counsel for Children, Denver, CO.: 1984.

26. Examples include: Alaska Stat. section 12.45.047 (1984); Ariz. Rev. Stat. Ann. section 12-2312 (1982); Ark. Stat. Ann. section 43-2036 (Supp. 1985); Cal. Penal Code section 1346 (Supp. 1985); Colo. Rev. Stat. section 18-3-413 (Supp. 1985); Fla. Stat. section 918.17 (1984); Ky. Rev. Stat. section 421.350 (1984); Me. Rev. Stat. Ann. tit. 15, section 1205 (Supp. 1984-85); Mont. Code Ann. section 46-15-401 (1983); N.M. Stat. Ann. section 30-9-17 (1978); N.Y.Cr.P.R. 190.32 (1985); S.D. Codified Laws Ann. section 23A-12-9 (Supp. 1984); Tex. Crim. Proc. Code Ann. section 38.071 (Supp. 1985); Wis. Stat. section 967.04(7) (1985).

27. U.S. Constitution Amendment VI.

28. *Ohio v. Roberts,* 448 U.S. 56,66 (1980).

29. G. Skoler, "New Hearsay Exceptions for a Child's Statement of Sexual Abuse," *The John Marshall Law Review* 18:1, 1984; J. Parker, "The Rights of Child Witnesses: Is the Court a Protector or a Perpetrator?" *New England Law Review* 17:643, 1982; G. J. Pierron, "A Comparative Analysis of Nine Recent State Statutory Approaches Concerning Special Hearsay Exceptions for Children's Out of Court Statements Concerning Sexual Abuse with Emphasis on What Constitutes Unavailability and Indicia of Reliability under *Ohio v. Roberts* and Other Decisions," in *Papers from a National Policy Conference on Legal Reforms in Child Sexual Abuse Cases,* American Bar Association, Washington, D.C.: 1985; M. H. Graham, "Child Sex Abuse Prosecutions: Hearsay and Confrontation Clause Issues," in *Papers from a National Policy Conference on Legal Reforms in Child Sexual Abuse Cases,* American Bar Association, Washington, D.C.: 1985.

30. Fed. R. Evid. 801(c).

31. *In re Penelope B.,* Wash. Sup. Ct., No. 50328-1, 12 F.L.R. 1080, 12-17-85.

32. Fed. R. Evid. 803(2); *U.S. v. Iron Shell,* 633 F.2d 77 (8th Cir. 1980), *cert. den.* 450 U.S. 1101 (1908); *U.S. v. Nick,* 604 F.2d 1199 (9th Cir. 1979); *Jackson v. State,* 419 So.2d 394 (Fla. App. 1982); *People v. Edgar,* 317 N.W.2d 675 (Mich. App. 1982); *Arvay v. State* 646 S.W.2d 320 (Tex. App. 1983).

33. *People in the Interest of O.E.P.,* 654 P.2d 312 (Colo. 1982); *Lancaster v. People,* 615 P.2d 720 (Colo. 1980); *Jackson v. State, supra; State v. Rodriguez,* 8 Kan. App. 2d 353, 657 P.2d 79 (1983); *People v. Edgar, supra.*

34. *Iron Shell, supra; Nick, supra; People v. Orduno,* 80 Cal. App.3d 738, 145 Cal. Rptr. 806 (1978).

35. *U.S. v. Napier,* 518 F.2d 316 (9th Cir. 1975), *cert. denied,* 423 U.S. 895 (1975).

36. Fed. R. Evid. 803(3); *In re Tanya P.,* 120 Cal. App.3d 66, 174 Cal. Rptr. 533 (1981); *People v. Pike,* 183 Cal. App. 2d 729, 7 Cal. Rptr. 188 (1960).

37. *In re Cheryl H.,* 153 Cal. App.3d 1098, 1131, 200 Cal. Rptr. 789, 810 (1984).

38. Fed. R. Evid. 803(4); *Iron Shell, supra; Nick, supra; State v. Hankins,* 612 S.W.2d 438 (Mo. App. 1981).

39. *Iron Shell, supra; Hankins, supra; Cartera v. Comm,* 248 S.E.2d 784 (Va. 1978).

40. *Goldade v. State* 647 P.2d 721 (Wyo. 1983).

41. Id. at 725.

42. *In the Matter of Angel R. and James R.,* State of Michigan Court of Appeals, No. 78059, June 10, 1985.

43. *People v. Wade*, 181 Cal. App.2d 314, 5 Cal. Rptr. 63 (1960); *Purdy v. State*, 343 So.2d 4 (Fla. 1977).

44. Examples include: Ariz. Rev. Stat. Ann. section 13-1416 (Supp. 1985); Colo. Rev. Stat. section 18-3-411(3) (Supp. 1985); Ill. Stat. Ann. Ch. 37, section 704-6(4)(c) (1985); Ind. Code section 35-37-4-6 (1985); Iowa Code Ann. section 232.96(6) (1985); Kan. Stat. Ann. section 60-460(dd) (1983); Minn. Stat. section 595.02(3) (Supp. 1985); S.D. Codified Laws Ann. section 19-16-38 (Supp. 1984); Utah Code Ann. section 76-5-411 (Supp. 1985); Wash. Rev. Code section 9A.44.120 (Supp. 1985-86).

45. Fed. R. Evid. 803(24).

46. Rule 803(24) has been adopted by: Alaska, Arizona, Arkansas, Colorado, Delaware, Hawaii, Iowa, Minnesota, Montana, Nebraska, New Mexico, North Dakota, Oklahoma, Oregon, South Dakota, Utah, Wisconsin, Wyoming.

47. Fed. R. Evid. 803(24).

48. Fed. R. Evid. 801(d)(2).

49. *In re Amos L.*, 124 Cal. App.3d 1031, 177 Cal. Rptr. 783 (1981).

50. Fed. R. Evid. 404(a).

51. Fed. R. Evid. 404(b); *State v. Lafleur*, 398 So.2d 1074 (La. 1981); *State v. Sutfield*, 354 So.2d 1334 (La. 1978).

52. *People v. Lint*, 182 Cal. App.2d 402, 6 Cal. Rptr. 95 (1960).

53. Fed. R. Evid. 404(b); *People v. Taggart*, 621 P.2d 1375 (Colo. 1981); *People v. Hosier*, 186 Colo. 116, 525 P.2d 1161 (1974).

54. Fed. R. Evid. 404(b); *State v. Foster*, 623 P.2d 1360 (Kan. 1981).

55. Fed. R. Evid. 404(b).

56. S. Johnson, "Trial Issues in Child Abuse," Unpublished, March 1982, p. 92.; *People v. Aeschlimann*, 28 Cal. App.3d 460, 104 Cal. Rptr. 689 (1972).

57. *People in the Interest of D.A.K.*, 596 P.2d 747 (Colo. 1979); *People in the Interest of C.R.*, 557 P.2d 1225 (Colo. App. 1976); *In re Cole*, 274 S.W.2d 601 (Mo. App. 1955).

PROTECTING CHILD WITNESSES

Donald C. Bross, J.D., Ph.D.

As greater efforts are undertaken to protect children from unlawful acts, issues of proof are likely to become more important, especially as these relate to the child as witness. Among the concerns are the degree to which children can be sheltered from testifying, the degree to which testimony is harmful and the degree to which child witnesses can be protected in the courtroom. Each of these issues is examined in turn from a legal perspective. Particular emphasis is given to the child sexual abuse victim.[1]

REASONS TO AVOID COURTROOM TESTIMONY BY CHILDREN

There are at least three reasons for not using children as witnesses. First, the child may be traumatized by the pretrial examination and preparation; the anxiety of waiting for the trial to occur; and the actual experience of being a witness, subject to examination, cross-examination, the scrutiny of judge, jurors and other adults in an exposed situation; and, in some instances, placed in the position of testifying against a loved one. Secondly, the judge may find the child legally incompetent, and thus he may not be allowed to testify after having gone through an ordeal of prior questioning and preparation for trial. Thirdly, the child's statements may not be credible or may be given little weight in the deliberations of the fact finder, whether the fact finder is a judge or a jury.

Each of these reasons may be inapplicable to a particular child or a particular case. Whatever the validity of these points, it makes sense to try and make the testimony of the child unnecessary. It is also possible that one or more of these concerns about a child's testimony may apply in a given case, making alternative means of proof essential.

DOCUMENTING A CASE FOR COURT
WITHOUT INTRODUCING A CHILD WITNESS

Some of the most serious offenses are unlikely to be witnessed. Murder cases and cases of treason, for example, are unlikely to be proven by eyewitnesses because of their secretive nature. Child abuse and crimes against children are often secretive harms. These cases, nevertheless, can be proven by direct and circumstantial evidence. Usually, it is the quality of the prosecution, the application of special skills and resources and the persistence of those concerned with the harm done that determine the outcome. Many means exist for proving child abuse cases without calling the children as witnesses. The excellence of investigation, diagnosis and evaluation,[2] as well as the courtroom presentation, are obviously crucial.

Statements by the Child Admitted as Hearsay

Increasingly, hearsay statements by child victims are being recognized as important sources of proof in child abuse.

Although statements in court about what another person has said to the witness are usually not admitted into evidence, important exceptions to the hearsay rule in child abuse cases include the excited or startled utterance, the medical exception to hearsay and admissions against interest.

These and other exceptions are delineated in the previous chapter on Evidentiary Issues.

Medical Findings

When examining possible victims of child sexual abuse, in particular, physicians frequently find no physical signs or symptoms, but with more attention being directed to the problem new indications of child sexual abuse are being discovered.[3] Sexually transmitted disease has been reported in as many as 13% of all possible cases of sexual abuse.[4] The important testimony from the physician may be, however, that in over 80 percent of all sexual abuse cases there are no such findings. Physical evidence such as hair, semen, blood and bitemarks may be present, but must be documented and, in the case of physical specimens, preserved in a "chain-of-evidence" which can satisfy the courts that there has been no tampering or likelihood of error in the evidence gathering process.

Developmental Information

Social workers, psychologists, teachers, physicians and others, to the extent that they are trained, experienced and perceptive about the ways ordinary children develop psycho-sexually, can provide important evidence of the observed behavioral differences in ordinary children and those thought to be sexually abused. The lay person's report of a child's inappropriate language and pseudosexual, emotionally promis-cuous and highly sexualized conduct can be given proper significance when a person with wide experience in dealing with ordinary children states how unusual such behavior is.

Evaluation of Alleged Perpetrator or Caretaker

Evaluation of those thought to have either harmed or failed a duty to protect the child raises several issues. While there may be patterns of sexually abusive parenting, innocence or guilt cannot be concluded by proof that the pattern does or does not exist.[5] If there are criminal charges, of course, evaluation will not be possible without the consent of the accused. Courts are somewhat divided in their rulings as to whether or not evaluations can be ordered in civil cases, but the better and more common rule appears to be that psychiatric evaluations can be ordered in civil abuse and neglect proceedings if relevancy can be established. The qualifications and experience of the evaluator are particularly important in this area. The best evidence that there is a problem may derive from the way that denial is presented. For example, in an incest case, it may be significant that many things about the children or the spouses' relationship is not discussed or cannot be discussed. The nonsexual aspects of family life may be little understood, remembered or of interest to the involved adult. The child advocate should be extremely wary of attempts to "rule out" sexual abuse based on polygraphs of the perpetrator.[6]

Evidentiary Innovations: Res Ipsa Loquitur

Recognition of the difficulties of proof have led to proposals that the doctrine of *res ipsa loquitur* be more frequently applied in civil proceedings on child abuse or neglect. The doctrine has been recognized in battering situations,[7] endorsed in the area of sexual abuse[8] and upheld in a tort action against a child care facility.[9] The doctrine recognizes that in some instances a victim may be unable to produce evidence of wrongful acts or omissions because control of the evidence is completely in the hands of the possible wrongdoer. It permits a court in a civil case to shift the burden for bringing forth certain evidence to the defendants. When a child suffers harm that cannot occur without unreasonable care or negligence, it requires those best able to show how the harm occurred to help achieve an explanation.

Through the use of *res ipsa loquitur* in civil cases of child sexual abuse, the following criteria have been suggested as sufficient to shift the burden of proof from the prosecution to the defense, who must provide evidence that the abuse did not occur. In prepubertal children, the burden should shift to the caretakers to show that the concerns are unjustified if, along with a clear statement by the child of sexual abuse, two or more of the following criteria exist:

1. Child develops neurasthenia symptoms without physiological basis, including: fatigue; weakness; headaches; bedwetting or excessive urination; stomachaches; ringing in the ear; sleeping, vasomotor, memory or concentration disturbances; or complaints of numerous and constantly varying aches.
2. Child expresses acting out behavior, including frequent masturbation and/or indiscriminate and pseudoseductive behavior.
3. Parent denies the action and has "blackout spells" due to excessive drinking; says children should be prepared for later sexual experiences; or, shows no concern and makes such statements as "All fathers do that", "If you raise a child, you should be able to do what you like with him", or "She's promiscuous anyway."
4. Physical evidence, via careful laboratory analyses, reveals semen or pubic hair on bedding or clothing at alleged scenes of incident.
5. Allegations are made by siblings of similar mistreatment.
6. Child assumes many parental responsibilities inappropriate for her/his age and family circumstances.

7. Medical evidence of sexual activity does not show that the child is sexually involved with anyone else.
8. Child expresses gender role confusion.
9. Parent is abnormally concerned about child's dating habits and social activities.[10]

Anatomically Correct Dolls

Younger children are often most comfortable using dolls to act out certain events.[11] To the extent that the child is preverbal, doll play may be the primary available means of symbolic communication. Adults required to interview child victims may themselves be more comfortable if the children use dolls to describe what happened to them. The behavior of the child can be narrated by a witness to the child's play, and this information may often be introduced in court without hearsay objections. As these techniques become more common, objections may increase. Then hearsay exceptions may have to be argued in order for the doll play to be admitted into evidence.

Audio and Videotaping

Preservation of the exact statements of a child's interview may be helpful to assure accuracy of hearsay statements and perhaps to support the admission of hearsay testimony. Any defects of memory can be minimized through the quick preservation of the child's information. New state statutes are experimenting with the preservation of children's statements through videotaped deposition. Under these statutes, there can be a ruling that a child is unavailable at trial for therapeutic reasons and thus, the earlier recorded statement should be admitted into evidence. The right to cross-examine and confront the witness can be preserved at the time of the deposition. There is more latitude to make the child witness comfortable with such an approach, and it permits the child to get through therapy and put the trauma behind without an impending trial.

REASONS TO INTRODUCE THE CHILD WITNESS

The Sexual Assault Center at Harborview Medical Center in Seattle, Washington, has been a pioneer in the introduction and protection of child witnesses. Their movie "Double Jeopardy", provides many examples of do's and don'ts for the investigator and prosecuting attorney alike. Within their framework, they argue that it is possible for many children to survive the process of testifying in court quite well and even to benefit from the vindication of having their complaints treated seriously, even if the verdict is not in their favor.

In many instances, there may be no way to prove a case without using the child as a witness. When the possible perpetrator is viewed as a serious risk to other children in care, or to children in the community as a whole, the fate of many children may rest on the degree to which a particular child victim or child witness can survive the trial experience.

Assumptions that children are not credible are being challenged.[12] About some other things, children may be more reliable than adults, and there is evidence that in many ways children are no different than adults, in that some recall events with more or less accuracy than others.

The Child Who Recants

At least two courts have recognized that sexually abused children may be pressured to change their stories or to recant what has originally been stated. One case relied primarily on evidence statutes[13] while the other recognized a "familial child sex abuse syndrome" which incorporates understanding of the pressures to recant.[14]

Supporting the Child Witness

From the moment that a child is first involved with authorities, the way that adults respond may determine both the iatrogenic harm done and the effectiveness of the child's testimony. Pressures to recant may be considerably reduced by appropriate placement and support, or support in the home, depending upon the identity of the perpetrator and the protectiveness of the parents.

Introduction to the courtroom can give the child witness some sense of the process, a feeling of some protection and control over her own involvement in the legal process, and perhaps alleviate some of the fear. The child can be advised of her rights, and advised either to avoid looking at those who frighten her in the courtroom or to look at those whom she trusts.

Courts are often willing and able to make protective orders, limiting who will be present or arranging the courtroom in a way that will be less threatening. There is obviously much more latitude in civil cases, and it is possible for the children to be interviewed only in chambers, perhaps only by the judge with a court recorder, and certainly in a closed courtroom.[15]

To the extent that the child's credibility is attacked, it will be possible to buttress the child's statements. An expert can consider the way in which a child's story has been unveiled in evaluating its degree of credibility. It appears from initial research that very few children have proven untruthful about many matters of sexual abuse.[16]

Guardian ad Litem or Child Advocate

While it is accepted and common practice to assign a guardian *ad litem* in civil cases of child abuse or neglect, it is much less common in criminal trials.[17] As an extension of victim and witness protection programs, it is time for prosecuting attorneys to consider using special trial assistants for the specific purpose of protecting the child witness, before, during, and after criminal trials. Among the duties of such specialists would be vigorous objection to confusing, intimidating and irrelevant cross-examination, and in general, speaking up for the child witness at trial.

In deciding whether or not a child witness must testify, an attorney will first have to review the record to see how well prior professionals have carried out their responsibilities. The attorney is likely to find that they have done a far better job if other professionals, in turn, have been trained by lawyers to know what is significant in the law and how to obtain and preserve that information. Children who have not had to repeat *in seriatum* a story to excessive numbers of people are much more likely to reveal the traumatic impact that the abuse has had on them. An attorney who is comfortable with children of different ages, and accustomed to their developmental differences, is much more likely to provide a child with the conditions he or she requires to survive, and even shine through, on the witness stand. The only satisfactory approach is case by case and child by child, without hard rules that require or disallow a given technique. No child deserves less.

FOOTNOTES

1. For a recent overview of legal developments on child sexual abuse, see: *Papers from a National Policy Conference on Legal Reforms in Child Sexual Abuse,* American Bar Association, Washington, D.C.: 1985.

See also Mary Avery, "The Child Witness: Potential for Secondary Victimization," *Criminal Justice Journal* 7:1, 1983; G. Skoler, "New Hearsay Exceptions for a Child's Statement of Sexual Abuse," *John Marshall Law Review* 18:1, 1984.

2. David P. H. Jones and Mary McQuiston, *Interviewing the Sexually Abused Child,* The C. Henry Kempe National Center, Denver, CO.: 1985.

3. H. B. Cantwell, "Vaginal Inspection as It Relates to Child Abuse in Girls Under Thirteen," *Child Abuse and Neglect* 7:171, 1983.

4. S. T. White, et al, "Sexually Transmitted Diseases in Sexually Abused Children," *Pediatrics* 72:16, 1983.

5. David P. H. Jones, personal communication, April 1984; *In re Cheryl H.*, 153 Cal. App.3d 1098, 200 Cal. Rptr. 789 (1984).

6. In *Illinois v. Starks* (Ill. Sup. Ct., April 9 1985) the prosecution was not allowed to renege on a plea bargain based on the defendant's favorable outcome on a polygraph, even though later independent evidence called into question the polygraph results.

7. *In re S.*, 66 Misc.2d 683, 322 N.Y.S.2d 170 (Fam. Ct. 1971).

8. J. Bulkley (ed.), *Child Sexual Abuse and the Law,* American Bar Association, Washington, D.C.: 1983, especially pp. 109-111.

9. *Zimmer v. Celebrities, Inc.*, 615 P.2d 76 (Colo. App. 1980).

10. S. Mele, "Parental Sexual Abuse of Children: The Law as a Therapeutic Tool for Families," in *Legal Representation of the Maltreated Child*, Donald C. Bross (ed.), National Association of Counsel for Children, Denver, CO.: 1979.

11. *State v. Lee*, 9 Ohio App.3d 282, 459 N.E.2d 910 (1983).

12. Gail Goodman, "The Child Witness: An Introduction," *Journal of Social Issues*, 40(2):1, 1984.

13. *In the Interest of K.A.J.*, 635 P.2d 921 (Colo. 1981).

14. *State v. Middleton*, 294 Or. 427, 657 P.2d 1215 (1983).

15. *State v. Sinclair*, 274 S.E.2d 411 (S.C. 1981).

16. For example, see studies cited by Mary Avery, *supra* note 1.

17. But see *State v. Walsh*, 495 A.2d 1256 (N.H. 1985).

EXPERTS IN CUSTODY CASES

Ann M. Haralambie, Esq.

HOW THE EXPERT CAN PREPARE THE ATTORNEY

As in all litigation employing experts, the attorney must be thoroughly briefed by the expert. The first use of an expert is in evaluating the case. Next the expert should be used in preparing for discovery. Naturally working with the expert during these phases will constitute a large measure of the expert's education of the attorney. This section will deal with additional pretrial preparation. The examples will involve mental health experts, but the principles are easily transferable to other types of experts.

The expert should provide the attorney with an analysis of the issues and facts relevant to his or her profession. For example, where one parent is alleged to be mentally ill, the attorney should understand the nature of the mental illness, how it affects parenting abilities, what treatment is available, how treatment will affect parenting abilities and the anticipated course and length of treatment. The expert should provide the attorney with a list of points the expert feels should be made and the significance of those points. One of the greatest

Reprinted with revisions from *Handling Child Custody Cases*, by Ann M. Haralambie, © 1983 by McGraw-Hill, Inc., by permission of Shepard's/McGraw-Hill. Further reproduction of any kind is strictly prohibited.

frustrations reported by expert witnesses is the failure of the attorneys to bring out the important information during the expert's testimony.

The mental health profession is often criticized for being too subjective, for being more art than science. Mental health testimony is subject to impeachment on cross-examination on this basis. One way to strengthen such opinion testimony is to show that there is empirical data to support the opinion. The expert must provide the attorney with this data by reference to standard texts, articles, research studies or psychological tests. It is equally important that the expert advise the attorney of any controverting data to avoid surprise at trial.

Just as the expert provides supporting information to buttress his or her opinion, information casting doubt on the opposing expert's opinion should be provided (with careful attention to information which supports the opinion). The attorney should ask the expert to label which data is widely accepted in the field and which is subject to differing opinion. Rarely should the attorney use supporting information that clearly represents a minority position unless it is the position of a substantial or influential minority. The expert must be willing to put aside his or her own loyalties in assessing the degree of acceptance of various viewpoints within the profession.

If the attorney will be asking his or her own expert hypothetical questions at trial, the expert should participate in constructing the hypothetical. The expert can also assist the attorney in preparing hypothetical questions for the opposing expert. In this way the questions will be meaningful within the witness's field of expertise.

In addition to preparing the attorney for making the most out of direct examination, the expert should prepare the attorney for cross-examining the opposing expert. The first step is an evaluation of the opposing expert's credentials. It is important to know the expert's theoretical orientation and type of practice. For example, an expert trained to counsel basically normal clients with family problems may not be sufficiently trained to diagnose or treat clients who are seriously mentally ill. An expert who engages in some bizarre form of therapy, such as nude encounter groups, is not likely to be accorded much credibility by the court.[1]

One's own expert should thoroughly review and critique the opposing expert's test data, evaluation methods and reports. The amount of time spent, extent of background information gathered, omissions and alternative explanations should be covered. With this information the attorney can demonstrate the weaknesses of the opposing expert during cross-examination and reiterate their significance during direct examination of the client's expert. Finally, the expert may be present during some or all of the trial testimony including that of the parties or opposing experts.[2] The expert may suggest cross-examination questions to the attorney while the opposing expert is testifying. Following the opposing expert's or opposing party's testimony the expert may suggest additional areas to be covered during his or her own testimony.

An attorney who is prepared for trial by the expert not only will be making more effective use of the expert, but also will be able to present a record for the trial court and appellate court which maximizes the effect of the expert information presented. In my practice the preparation my experts have given me has been at least as important to the outcome of the case as has been my trial preparation of the experts.

HOW TO PREPARE THE EXPERT FOR TRIAL

The process of preparing the expert for trial should begin upon selecting the expert. This section deals with the specific preparation for the art of testifying.[3] The attorney must first determine whether the expert is an experienced witness who is at ease on the witness stand. An expert who understands his or her role in the decision-making process and the methodology of trial will be far more relaxed.[4]

The expert should understand that his or her role is to provide and interpret information for the judge, who will evaluate that information and, with consideration of the other evidence at trial, make the final decision. An expert whose recommendation is not followed has not failed and should not assume that his or her expertise was lightly regarded. An expert who understands what information is needed and how it fits into the attorney's case, will feel comfortable with direct examination. Similarly, an expert who understands the methods and purposes of impeachment and who anticipates the type of questions to be asked, will not feel personally attacked or ridiculed during cross-examination.

The attorney should explain the difference between the purposes of direct and cross-examination and the difference in ways of answering. For example, because leading questions are not permitted during direct examination, the attorney may ask what seem to be unduly vague questions. If the expert knows what information he or she is expected to provide, the purpose of the questions will be more readily ascertained, and the witness will not need to ask the embarrassing question, "What are you trying to get at?" Direct examination questions are usually open-ended, allowing the witness to elaborate on an answer. The witness should know that a certain amount of elaboration is permitted.

Cross-examination, on the other hand, is typified by short questions which call for direct, limited answers, often "yes" or "no." The expert needs to understand that "putting words into the witness's mouth" is the essence of good cross-examination and a perfectly acceptable technique. The witness should not be defensive about the technique or be lulled into the rhythm of a good cross-examiner, thereby giving an erroneous answer. The witness must listen carefully to the question and give an accurate, but short, answer unless the attorney or judge requests elaboration.

The most important attribute a witness can have is objectivity. For this reason, the expert should not become an advocate; rather, he or she should allow the attorney to advocate based on the testimony given. The witness's demeanor should remain the same, regardless of which attorney is doing the questioning. The distinction is a crucial one which should be emphasized to the witness even to the point of rehearsing the style of testimony if it is too adversarial. The expert should readily concede weaknesses in the client's position and limitations in the expert's data base or evaluation procedures. This should be done with professional impartiality, not with an air of regret at having to admit the weakness.

One common ploy on cross-examination is to say to the witness, "You're being paid by the plaintiff to testify here, aren't you?" The expert should reply that payment is being made for the time spent in making the evaluation and for the time spent away from the office during testimony. Because few custody matters are tried to a jury, and judges are well aware that experts paid for their time are not necessarily providing "bought testimony," this ploy is a cheap shot which reflects more on opposing counsel than on the expert. However, I have seen experts answer the question with such defensiveness and resentment that they never regained an objective demeanor.

Many attorneys engage in expert-baiting, a dangerous tactic for both attorney and expert. The expert who is widely respected in his or her own field may be treated with insults, innuendo and demeaning remarks if counsel and the judge permit it. It is extremely important for the expert not to lose control. The witness should not spar with the attorney or engage in debate. The attorney must warn the witness in advance that opposing counsel may resort to such techniques and must explain that counsel will do so in an attempt to make the expert lose poise on the stand, thereby weakening the impact of the testimony. Such tactics are resorted to most frequently when opposing counsel has no good reply to the substantive testimony. Once the expert understands the game, it will be easier to resist the temptation to play. Of course, the attorney owes it to the witness to object if opposing counsel's questioning gets out of hand.

One of the most frustrating aspects of cross-examination for experts is the questioning attorney's instruction to "answer the question yes or no." Sometimes a question is easily susceptible of such an answer (*e.g.*, "Did you read the mother's hospital records?"). Other times, it cannot be answered yes or no at all. In such cases, the witness should explain that such an answer is not possible. Most cases fall somewhere in the middle. If such an answer is possible but misleading, the witness may state that to the judge. Frequently, the judge will direct the witness to explain. If not, the witness has alerted counsel for the need to explain on redirect examination. Used sparingly, one technique I have had witnesses use is the "but, yes" answer instead of the "yes, but" format, putting the qualification before the dogmatic answer. The two examples below illustrate the difference:

Q. Don't you feel that John, in his mother's custody, is an undisciplined boy?

["Yes, but" format]

A. Yes, but. . . .
Q. Thank you, that answers the question.

["But, yes" format]

A. To the extent that most adolescents are rebellious, yes.

I have found that witnesses easily become adept at this maneuver, and if the qualification is kept short, opposing counsel rarely has time to cut off further answer. It is important, however, to caution the witness that overuse of this technique becomes objectionable game-playing which may warrant a direct admonition from the judge to answer yes or no.

The expert should understand that if he or she acknowledges the authoritativeness of a treatise, it can be used for impeachment. Therefore, the expert should be instructed to deny, if appropriate, or narrow the scope of the author's agreed-upon competence when presented with such an inquiry during cross-examination.

The attorney should not only advise the expert of the substantive issues to be addressed (and perhaps actual questions) on direct examination and the likely topics of cross-examination, but he or she should also consider taking the witness through a mock examination and cross-examination. I thoroughly enjoy role-playing the part of opposing counsel and try to imitate that particular attorney's style. While answers should not be rehearsed and memorized, the attorney should point out weaknesses in the way questions are answered and offer alternative examples for illustrative purposes. The witness should understand the question before answering. He or she should be instructed that it is proper to ask the attorney to break down multiple questions or to restate a question to make sure that it is correctly understood. It may be helpful to provide the expert with a written list of witness tips and to go over the list during the pre-trial preparation.

QUALIFYING THE EXPERT

According to most state rules of evidence, relatively little is needed to qualify a witness as an expert. Federal Rules of Evidence, Rule 702, upon which many state rules are patterned, provides

> If scientific, technical, or other specialized knowledge will assist the trier of fact to understand the evidence or to determine a fact in issue, a witness qualified as an expert by knowledge, skill, experience, training, or education, may testify thereto in the form of an opinion or otherwise.

Most experts used at trial possess considerably more qualifications than those minimally needed to meet the requirements for opinion testimony. Where opposing parties present their own experts, the credentials of each witness become particularly important. The question then becomes how to present the witness's credentials.

Perhaps the worst technique, and the most common, is to ask the witness, "Please state your credentials." The expert is then put in the position of either pompously extolling his or her own virtues or modestly ignoring the very qualifications which will enhance the testimony. A better practice is for the attorney to ask short, direct questions covering education, postgraduate training, professional positions, length of time in practice, publications, teaching positions, connection with governmental organizations, professional honors and affiliations and previous experience as an expert witness.[5] The attorney should always ask the expert for an up-to-date resume or curriculum vitae for use in qualifying the witness. It is better for the attorney to have too much information, from which he or she may choose, than to miss an important credential which would greatly enhance the expert's credibility or the weight to be accorded to the expert's testimony.

The qualification stage of testimony should not be rushed through as a formality, and unless the judge is very familiar with the expert (as often happens in juvenile court), the attorney should not automatically accept the opposing party's offer to stipulate to the witness's expertise.

Careful consideration should be given to the issues in the trial and the expert's particular qualifications to address those issues. For example, in a domestic relations custody dispute where there are allegations of abuse, I emphasize the fact that my witness is on contract to do evaluations for child protective services and testifies frequently in juvenile court abuse cases. Similarly, I point out that my expert teaches a class in parenting skills and coauthored a book on parenting. Many attorneys do not realize that most psychologists and psychiatrists do not treat many abuse cases in their private practices unless they are in some way affiliated with child protective services or hospitals. By establishing the experience of one's own witness in abuse cases, impeachment of the opposing expert who does not have such experience will be more effective.

DIRECT EXAMINATION

Effective direct examination is predicated upon the attorney's substantive preparation and the witness's trial preparation by the attorney. The expert must be prepared for direct examination. This may require an actual question by question practice session, a list of questions to be asked or merely a discussion of topics to be covered. The expert should know the different purposes and techniques of direct and cross-examination. It is very important that the expert understand what the attorney needs to prove. By knowing what must be proved and what information must be provided through his or her testimony, the expert will be able to understand the nonleading (sometimes vague and awkward) direct examination questions.

The first step in the direct examination is to qualify the witness as an expert who may give opinion testimony. The judge may need to be educated about the witness's field in order to properly understand what his or her qualifications really are. Then the witness's contacts with the case should be explored. The judge needs to know how often the expert has seen the party, how much time has been spent, the circumstances and nature of the contacts, and what additional sources of information were used. After showing what the examination consisted of, the attorney should ask the expert to explain what the examination has revealed.

If the expert's opinion includes a diagnosis, the diagnosis should be related to the custodial or visitation abilities of the party. Negative points about the client must be dealt with forthrightly, a painful process which not only "draws the sting out" of a cross-examination question, but also adds to the expert's credibility as an impartial and objective professional. It is helpful for the expert to explain what the client's parenting potential and capacity for change are. The expert can outline a plan for therapy or environmental changes which will effect that change.

The witness should generally be asked to state the basis for his or her opinion, giving the expert an opportunity to elaborate on his or her answer. Most evidentiary rules allow an expert to base an opinion on inadmissible evidence if it is of a type reasonably relied upon by other experts in the field.[6] The expert may state the reasons for his or her opinion without revealing the underlying facts.[7] During cross-examination the expert may be required to disclose those facts.[8] The witness should be able to articulate the areas involved in his or her judgment and the manner in which the conclusions were reached. The language that the expert uses should not be overloaded with jargon and technical terms. On the other hand, enough technical terminology must be used to show that the witness is speaking in the context of an accepted field of expertise and to create an adequate and precise record on appeal. I suggest to my expert witnesses that they use the technical terms where appropriate, defining them within the sentence. The expert's tone is important, lest the definitions become patronizing or pedantic.

Without allowing the witness to merely ramble in a long narrative fashion, the attorney should ask open-ended questions that give the expert an opportunity to educate the court about the situation. Experienced witnesses acquire a feel for how long an answer should continue and pause periodically to allow the attorney to pose another question. An attorney should always run through a brief, mock direct examination with a witness he or she has not heard testify. This practice will avoid the embarrassing situation at trial of having the witness constantly admonished to wait for another question or having the witness repeatedly ask, "What are you getting at?"

Where the expert's recommendation goes against his or her general bias, that should be brought out during direct examination. For example, in a divorce modification case where I represent the noncustodial parent, I have the expert state his or her general philosophy and practice of supporting the continuity of care by the custodial parent. The impact of the recommendation to change custody is then much stronger.

One problem that often arises with mental health experts who have interviewed the children is the question of whether the children have reported events accurately to the expert. Often, if asked the right question, the witness can demonstrate alternative explanations. For example, I once represented a noncustodial father who was seeking custody of his two young daughters. The children reported a pattern of neglectful incidents, which were corroborated by other witnesses. While our petition to modify the divorce decree was pending, the girls reported an increasing stream of threats from their mother against their step-mother and three-year-old step-brother. After one incident I advised the father, who had temporary custody, to take the children to the psychologist who was evaluating them. The children told the psychologist that their mother had a gun in the car, that she told them she was going to take them to California and that she was going to shoot their step-brother. At trial the mother vehemently denied the entire incident. I had the psychologist testify about what the children had reported and their reactions.[9] She further testified that in separate interviews the children gave identical accounts, although in different language. The girls were quite upset by the incident, and she stated that, if the incident had happened as reported, there was a serious question raised about the mother. The next question, however, brought out an important point.

Q.   Although you have testified that you believed the girls, assume for now that the incident never happened at all, or that the girls misperceived the facts. Would you have any opinion concerning the fact that the girls gave you those reports?

A.   Yes. In order for them to have fabricated such a story, especially in such detail, their relationship with their mother would have to be seriously disturbed.

The effect of that question was that whether the incident ever happened or not, there were real problems with the mother and her parenting of the girls.

I have been in a number of situations where such alternative explanations were possible, and when given, were devastating. Wherever there is a question about the truth of a child's allegations about the parent, the mental health expert should give such alternative opinions.

CROSS-EXAMINATION

The attorney planning to cross-examine an expert should be well studied in the proper techniques for cross-examination. Numerous books cover the subject in detail, and one should start by reading at least one.[10] In addition, there are a number of books and articles on cross-examining mental health professionals in custody cases.[11] The legal commonplace that the best cross-examination of an expert may be no cross-examination should be considered, especially if the attorney has not deposed the expert or otherwise discovered information indicating that the witness will admit specific and helpful information. That advice notwithstanding, I have never passed up an opportunity to cross-examine an expert witness in a custody case, and I particularly enjoy cross-examining social workers and psychologists. The key, as always, is preparation.

The primary purpose of cross-examination is to obtain information that will directly help one's own case. The attorney should secure from the witness any information which tends to show that his or her own client is a good or adequate parent or that the opposing party has weaknesses as a parent. If the opposing party is the state or a private agency, the expert may be willing to testify about gaps in the case management or weaknesses in the case plan. In some cases the expert may be able to testify that the course of conduct by the agency diluted the parental ties or interfered with the family unnecessarily, such as by providing more supportive services to the foster family than to the natural family. If nothing else, the witness may be able to qualify the client's own expert or to concede the authoritativeness of treatises that support the client's contentions. In seeking to obtain any type of admission, the attorney must pay heed to the admonition not to ask a question to which the answer is not known.

The secondary purpose of cross-examination is impeachment. There are several areas of impeachment: the witness's training and experience, limited data base, theoretical rationale, choice of methods or treatment, bias or actual dishonesty. The last category will rarely be encountered and, therefore, will not be covered here. All of the remaining categories seek to impeach either the witness's credentials, data, or findings.

I have a stylistic aversion to attorneys who cross-examine in a snide and generally disrespectful manner. It appears to be counterproductive in almost all cases. The same information and concessions can usually be obtained by treating the witness with the same respect one accords his or her own expert. In addition, it is easier to catch a witness off-guard if one is polite.

Impeachment should usually proceed with the least threatening areas first. For example, most witnesses would be more willing to concede weaknesses in data than in credentials or findings. Therefore, one early impeachment question might be, "Doctor, since you have not had an opportunity to interview or evaluate my client, you are not making any kind of comparison or recommendation between the parents, are you?" Demonstrating limitations of the data base should be done in almost every case, beginning with the expert's inability to see crucial parties and continuing with the expert's inability or failure to communicate with other witnesses having useful information, to review other available evidence, or to follow up on other suggested avenues of information. Mental health experts rarely see their function as that of investigator of all possible sources of information, even though they will concede that more information is always helpful in arriving at accurate findings.

An expert's findings are only as good as the data upon which they are based, and by impeaching the data base, the findings are automatically brought into question. At this point, the attorney may want to raise a series of hypothetical questions relating to other information that is either in evidence already or will be introduced. The expert may be asked if such evidence is consistent with what he or she was told or would have predicted. The expert may also be asked whether such information, had it been known, would have affected the expert's conclusions or treatment. The attorney should carefully consider whether to ask such questions, however, unless it is clear that the witness would testify that it would have an effect or unless the nature of the evidence is such that if the witness testifies it would have no effect, the witness would lose all credibility. An example of the latter situation would be where a counselor testifies that his opinion that the father would be an appropriate custodian for his daughter would not change if he knew that in fact the father was having an ongoing sexual relationship with the girl. Finally, the expert's findings may be attacked because of incomplete or incorrect interpretation of the data. This type of impeachment must be backed up by controverting expert testimony.

Impeaching an expert based on his or her credentials is done in three situations: where the witness has limited experience, where the general nature of the expert's qualifications is limited and where the particular qualifications are lacking. The first situation occurs where the expert is properly qualified by training but has had little experience with custody cases or with the particular type of mental illness or emotional disturbance involved in the case. An example of the second situation arose in a case where a psychologist was arguing that physical correlates for a learning disability had not been ruled out, and therefore, she would not diagnose the child as learning disabled. She was adamant that the girl was not, in fact, learning disabled, even though a medical doctor had ruled out the physical correlates and made a diagnosis of learning disability. I had the psychologist admit her lack of training or other qualifications to overrule the physician's medical diagnosis. The third situation is more difficult and necessarily involves a more personal attack on the witness. In such impeachment the attorney would demonstrate that the expert had some type of inferior schooling, bizarre or generally unaccepted training or had failed professional certification or other indicia of professional excellence. This type of impeachment also requires, in most cases, testimony from one's own expert.

PSYCHOLOGICAL TESTING INSTRUMENTS

There are hundreds of psychological (psychometric) tests. Some are widely used, and others are not. Where psychologists are involved in custody cases, psychometric tests are likely to be part of the evaluation process. Various types of professionals have different backgrounds and training in administering and interpreting test results, and the attorney must inquire about the competence of the experts involved to testify about such results. Generally, clinical psychologists are the only professionals with significant training and skill in all types of psychometric tests. Other professionals are trained to administer and interpret only certain types of psychometric tests. Tests used as the basis for expert testimony should be used widely in the profession, the norms should be standardized for the population to whom they are being applied and the tests should be validated for the purposes for which they are used. If a test does not satisfy this three-pronged analysis, the attorney should seek to exclude testimony based on the test or to impeach the weight to be given such testimony.

Standardized tests compare the test-taker's answers with those of other persons. Therefore, it is important that the standard group be fairly representative. The attorney should ask the expert about the population from which the norms were established—it has amazed me how few psychologists can answer that question. Some tests have never been standardized. Some tests are standardized to a very small or racially skewed sample. The attorney should inquire about the mean and the standard deviation of test results and whether the test has been revised. If there has been a revision, ask the expert whether the revised version was administered. An attorney willing to do some homework concerning a test that has been used will often uncover a wealth of cross-examination material.

An example of the standardization of a test is the Minnesota Multiphasic Personality Inventory (MMPI),[12] a widely used personality test which suggests personality traits and such mental disorders as paranoia, schizophrenia and depression. The MMPI was administered to patients in a mental institution in Minnesota. These patients had been diagnosed as having various mental illnesses and abnormal tendencies. The test was standardized by analyzing the answers to certain questions given by people who were depressed, compulsive, etc.[13] Therefore, if the person being tested answers the questions the way the schizophrenic patients did, the person is considered to be schizophrenic. This explanation is oversimplified, but it demonstrates one method of standardization. Such tests can be attacked on the ground that what they tell about the population used to set the norm cannot be applied to other test-takers. If they are not normed for a minority population, they cannot be applied to minorities.[14] Good psychologists never rely on the results of such tests alone, always checking for consistent results from other tests, clinical interviews and behavioral observations. No one test, standing alone, is particularly useful.

There are several intelligence tests, the most widely used being the Weschler Adult Intelligence Scale[15] and the Weschler Intelligence Scale for Children-Revised.[16] These tests are comprised of separately scored subtests, which measure various aspects of intelligence and thought disorders. The subtests fall within two categories, verbal and performance. The combined subtest scores yield Verbal IQ and Performance IQ scores, which are then combined again to yield a Full-Scale IQ score. Weschler and others have written about the use to be made of subtest scores and the discrepancy between such scores. If an expert testifies concerning the implications of subtest discrepancies, it is important for the attorney to know whether the discrepancy has been validated for the conclusions being drawn by the expert.

Projective tests, such as the Rorschach ink blot test,[17] are very subjectively interpreted. In a projective test the test-taker explains what various pictures or situations look like or mean to him or her. While the explanations may suggest certain personality characteristics or psychological traits, they are not conclusive. An expert relying solely on projective tests is very vulnerable during cross-examination because of the limited nature of the test results and the lack of standard responses. When confronted with unfavorable testimony based on a Rorschach, the attorney might want to subpoena the test cards and ask the expert to explain why the particular responses show some particular problem. Responses on the Rorschach or other projective tests, such as the Thematic Apperception Test (TAT)[18] and Children's Apperception Test (CAT),[19] may be less reliable when administered to highly creative people, whose unusual responses may be a function of their creativity rather than personality traits or emotional disturbances.

A growing field is neuropsychology, which studies organic brain damage. A well-trained neuropsychologist may be able to diagnose organic impairment (organicity) that is not picked up by a psychiatrist or neurologist. The leading group of neuropsychological tests is the Halstead–Reitan Neuropsychological Test Battery. The attorney should make sure that any expert who testifies concerning organicity is properly qualified and has administered the appropriate tests. Much is being written in the area, but few experts are truly qualified to make neuropsychological diagnoses.

Assuming that the tests used are accepted, standardized and validated, the attorney should ascertain whether they were administered according to the instructions provided with the tests. Standardized tests are always accompanied by detailed instructions on how the test should be administered and scoring manuals on how the results should be tabulated and interpreted. More often than one might expect, the tests are not administered or interpreted according to the instructions. Many practitioners develop their own procedures for administering and interpreting psychometric tests. Even if the test has been validated for the purpose for which it is being used, the validation rests on proper administration and scoring. Conclusions based on an improperly used test are not entitled to the same weight as those based on a properly used test, and the credibility of an expert who has not properly administered or interpreted a test is thereby diminished.

Psychological testimony is greatly enhanced by the use of psychometric tests. They lend support to the expert's clinical impressions and often provide additional evidence of the parties' strengths and weaknesses. The attorney should exploit their use by having his or her own expert explain the tests used and their significance. On cross-examination the attorney should dilute the impact of the other party's expert by demonstrating weaknesses in the tests used, the method of administration, and the validity of the conclusions reached. One's own expert can be very helpful in providing the information necessary to deal with the use of psychometric tests during both direct and cross-examination.

SHOWING ABUSE OR NEGLECT

Custody cases involving parental unfitness based on abuse or neglect of the child must be handled in a special way. The attorney handling such a case should become familiar with some of the leading works in the field. Expert assistance and testimony are particularly important in abuse and neglect cases, because it is one field where the truth is often counterintuitive. For example, most abusers really love their children, and many abused children are affectionate with and show no fear of the abuser. Often, they feel that the abuse is deserved punishment. Similarly, the normal response of a child who is being molested by a parent is to say nothing about the molestation. The offender and victim may have what appears to be a very close and loving relationship, even though the child may hate the sexual involvement. It is precisely in those cases where common sense is empirically wrong that expert testimony is essential.[20]

The first issue that must be addressed is what constitutes abuse. The line between permissible discipline and physical abuse is difficult to draw and subject to wide variation based on upbringing, socioeconomic status and cultural perspective.[21] The cultural differences are only recently being acknowledged on a widespread basis.[22] While experts can and should explain why certain behaviors are abusive, it is generally the judge's own definitions of abuse that ultimately decide the case.

Physicians can testify about medical diagnoses that relate specifically to physical abuse and neglect. For example, there is a recognized diagnosis of "battered child syndrome,"[23] which describes one type of physical abuse pattern. The term has a specific meaning and should not be applied to all cases of physical abuse, even those occurring over a long period of time.

Parents who physically abuse their children often take them to different doctors and hospitals for each injury to avoid detection. State child protection agencies have access to central registries which can help find records of various hospitalizations where abuse is suspected. This pattern is an accepted indicator of physical abuse within the medical, mental health, and law enforcement fields.

Physicians are usually necessary witnesses in cases involving inflicted injury (nonaccidental trauma). Most parents who have physically abused their children provide a superficially plausible explanation for how the child was accidentally injured. There is rarely a witness to the injury who is available to testify. A lay person is not equipped to judge whether a spirally fractured arm was caused by a fall from a swing or a wrenching blow by the parent. Physicians, especially if they are forensic pathologists or are involved in hospital pediatrics, may be able to explain the inconsistency between the parent's explanation and the physical evidence. For example, a two-month-old child does not have the motor ability to move across a bed and fall off, breaking a bone. A physician can rule out the parent's explanation and, generally, alternative explanations suggested by the parent's attorney. Parents rarely have the specialized knowledge necessary to fabricate an explanation for the injury which will be entirely consistent with the physical evidence.

Forensic pathologists are frequently considered as witnesses only where a person has died and the pathologist has performed an autopsy. However, forensic pathologists can be extremely helpful in proving physical abuse. They are generally better trained at determining the cause of injury than the pediatrician. In one of my cases a girl had been scalded by the parents. The mother testified that the girl got into a too-hot bath while bathing herself. The forensic pathologist and a police child abuse detective went to the house to measure the temperature and flow of the water. The pathologist and reconstructive surgeon, a burn expert, noted the burn patterns and splash marks on the girl. They were able to calculate how long she would have been in contact with the water and at what angle her body would have been. With that information, we were able to prove that the girl was held in the water (based on the burn patterns) for a longer period of time than she could have stood the water by herself (based on the water temperature and depth of the burns, coupled with the pathologist's knowledge of how long a similarly situated child would have been able to stay in contact with water of that temperature). Not only was the testimony impressive to the trial court, but it also made an excellent record on appeal. Pathologists can frequently describe what instrument or type of instrument was used to inflict injury, the age of various injuries, the amount of force necessary to cause the injury and the direction from which the force was applied.

Radiologists are extremely helpful witnesses in cases of multiple fractures in different stages of healing (one situation frequently encountered in battered child syndrome cases). A routine hospital procedure in cases of suspected nonaccidental trauma is the taking of a complete set of x-rays. If the x-rays show fractures in various stages of healing, there is a likelihood of systematic physical abuse (most children do not break bones accidently on several occasions). The attorney, as a precaution, should ask the pediatrician to rule out any type of brittle bone disease for children suffering from multiple fractures. Radiologists can also detect growth arrest patterns on x-rays, which show that the child has been malnourished or starved at different times in the past.

There is also a recognized diagnosis of failure-to-thrive, which describes a situation where an infant or young child fails to grow and gain weight as expected even though there is no physical reason for the failure. The actual cause is the caretaker's emotional abuse or neglect of the child. The diagnosis is confirmed by admitting the child to the hospital, where he or she is given appropriate care and fed properly, subsequently gaining weight rapidly. Failure to gain weight in the hospital setting will usually rule out the diagnosis. Testimony from a pediatrician can establish this type of abuse or neglect.

Physicians and public health nurses can be useful in documenting a parent's failure to provide necessary or adequate medical care for the child. The expert should explain to the court not only what steps the parent should have taken and why, but also whether typical parents would have taken some action. It is sometimes difficult for parents to know when medical attention is needed; therefore, if the family doctor gave the parent explicit instructions that were not carried out, the court will have more reason for concern than in a situation where the parent did not realize that leaving an earache unattended could result in deafness. In medical neglect cases, it is important to explore the parent's willingness to obtain appropriate knowledge through classes, books or visits by a public health nurse. If such services have been offered, the attorney should investigate whether or not the parent followed through on the training and took appropriate action thereafter.

If it is difficult to define the limits of physical abuse, it is even more difficult to define emotional or psychological abuse. As is the case with physical abuse cases, the standard that will ultimately be applied is likely to be the judge's personal standard. However, the attorney should present mental health testimony concerning what the abuse was and, most importantly, what effect it has had and will have on the child. The parent's willingness to cooperate in remedying the situation is an important issue in deciding whether the child would remain with that parent. More important, however, is a detailed analysis of the child's current needs and the present ability of the parent to meet those needs. Sometimes emotionally abused or neglected children need a time away from the parent for healing. On the other hand, sometimes the greatest need is to be with that parent under controlled circumstances, such as a placement with the parent conditioned on family and individual counseling. If sufficient indicators exist, the mental health expert might be able to predict the likelihood of future adequate parenting and set out an appropriate treatment plan.

Child abuse and neglect cases almost always include testimony by social workers. Most social workers called to testify as expert witnesses have Masters of Social Work degrees. Social workers are trained to evaluate and treat families in the context of their environment. They can assess the parties' community and family support systems, ability to function in the society and individual strengths and weaknesses. Social workers can also provide direct therapy and referral to private and public agencies. If family stress is caused by environmental factors, such as unemployment or inadequate daycare, the social worker can seek solutions. Social workers, especially those in child protective services, frequently have more direct training and experience in child abuse and neglect cases than other available experts. When such experts are available, the attorney should always consult with them and consider using them as witnesses. The attorney should be sure to qualify the witness properly, including eliciting testimony concerning the training social workers receive and exactly what expertise is encompassed by the profession.

Because judges sometimes undervalue the expertise of social workers, the attorney should use treatises to bolster the witness's testimony. This is an especially useful technique for the child's attorney, who usually questions the witness under the rules of cross-examination. The treatises used by social workers are often written by physicians or psychologists and are based on significant statistical data.

In many abuse cases there are two parties who, for all practical purposes, are on the same side with respect to an expert. For example, the child's attorney and the state's attorney might both view an expert witness as helpful and not to be impeached. Where one attorney calls the expert as a witness, the other is free to cross-examine, using leading questions and, most importantly, inquiring into the basis for the expert's opinion. Attorneys in such a situation may take what I call the "conspiratorial approach" to examination of the expert. Where time must be saved, the attorney who calls the expert may want to elicit only brief testimony, allowing the other attorney to move through the testimony more quickly by asking leading questions. Of the greater importance, however, is the cross-examining attorney's ability to elicit otherwise inadmissible evidence to show the basis for the expert's opinion.[24] In addition to revealing important statements that might otherwise be considered hearsay, for example, the attorney may make extensive use of treatises to bolster the expert's testimony.

USE OF TREATISES

Local law differs considerably on the use of treatises. Most courts hold that in the absence of statutory authority treatises are not admissible as independent evidence of the facts stated therein;[25] however, treatises may often be used during the cross-examination of experts.[26] For example, if the expert testifies that he or she has used a treatise in forming an opinion in the case which was expressed during direct examination, that particular treatise may be used.[27] Many courts also permit use of treatises where the expert has relied on the author's works, even though that particular treatise was not specifically used as a basis for the opinions elicited during direct examination.[28] Some courts permit use of treatises where the expert concedes the authoritativeness of the treatise, even though he or she has not personally relied on it.[29] Finally, some courts will permit use of treatises if any expert who has testified has established the authoritativeness of the treatise.[30]

The federal courts have adopted the more liberal view. Rule 803(18) of the Federal Rules of Evidence, after which many state evidence codes are patterned, provides for an exception to the hearsay rule for learned treatises:

> To the extent called to the attention of an expert witness upon cross-examination or relied upon him in direct examination, statements contained in published treatises, periodicals, or pamphlets on a subject of history, medicine, or other science or art, established as a reliable authority by the testimony or admission of the witness or by other expert witness or judicial notice. If admitted, the statements may be read into evidence but may not be received as exhibits.

Jurisdictions following the federal rule allow the treatises to be used substantively even if the expert neither relied on the treatise nor conceded its authoritativeness. Further, counsel may use treatises to bolster his or her own witness's testimony on direct examination by having the witness establish the reliability of the treatise, periodical or pamphlet.

The key to the use of treatises and other publications is establishing their authoritativeness, either by the witness personally or, if permitted by local law, by an expert.[31] Unless the work is considered to be authoritative, no court will permit its use.

During direct examination, treatises are used to add weight to the expert's opinion. This is particularly important where the witness's credentials are not as good as those of the opposing expert or where the court does not consider the witness's field of expertise to be very reliable. Because courts often underrate social workers, I make extensive use of treatises when examining them.

During cross-examination, treatises may be used to show a number of things. For example, where the expert has relied upon the particular treatise, any inconsistencies between what the expert has testified to and what the treatise says may be used for impeachment. Where the witness has conceded the authoritativeness of the treatise or the author, that person's views may be presented through the treatise or article. If the expert refuses to acknowledge the authoritativeness of works that other experts have established as well-accepted in the field, that witness's credibility may be diminished. I once showed that a witness in a child abuse case could not be an expert in that field if he had never heard of two of the foremost experts in the area, Drs. C. Henry Kempe and Ray Helfer, and had not read any of their writings.

Because of the subjective nature of many custody and visitation cases, treatises and articles may be very helpful in adding authority to the testimony of one's own witnesses and position and impeaching the opposing party's experts and position.

The DSM-III

An essential book for anyone dealing with mental disorders is the Diagnostic and Statistical Manual of Mental Disorders

(DSM-III), 1980, third edition, published by the American Psychiatric Association. This book represents the most recent classification of mental disorders and is widely used by psychiatrists, psychologists and counselors who make diagnoses. Disorders are arranged by categories, and within the categories, specific disorders are described and assigned a diagnostic number. Each category is explained in general terms, and each specific disorder is described according to essential features, associated features, predisposing factors and other parameters.[32] Some disorders are further broken down into subtypes.

The most useful features for the attorney are the diagnostic criteria and differential diagnosis sections. Psychiatric and psychological evaluations frequently contain the DSM-III diagnosis number. This will key the attorney into the book. For example, 313.21 is "Avoidant Disorder of Childhood or Adolescence." The diagnostic criteria are

A. Persistent and excessive shrinking from contact with strangers.
B. Desire for affection and acceptance, and generally warm and satisfying relations with family members and other familiar figures.
C. Avoidant behavior sufficiently severe to interfere with social functioning in peer relationships.
D. Age at least 2½. If 18 or older, does not meet the criteria for Avoidant Personality Disorder.
E. Duration of the disturbance of at least six months.[33]

The following are given as differential diagnoses.

> *Socially reticent* children are slow to warm up to strangers, but after a short time can respond, and suffer no impairment in peer interaction.
>
> In *Separation Anxiety Disorder*, the anxiety is due to separation from the home or major attachment figures rather than to contact with strangers per se. In *Overanxious Disorder*, anxiety is not limited to, or focused on, contact with strangers. In

Schizoid Disorder of Childhood or Adolescence there is also discomfort in social situations, but there is little desire for social involvement, whereas in Avoidant Disorder of Childhood or Adolescence there is a clear desire for affection and acceptance. *Avoidant Personality Disorder,* rather than Avoidant Disorder of Childhood or Adolescence, should be diagnosed only if the behavioral pattern has existed for many years and the individual is at least 18 years old. In *Adjustment Disorder with Withdrawal,* the behavioral pattern of withdrawal is clearly related to a recent psychosocial stressor.[34]

Most experts who testify do not expect to be examined on the specifics of reaching the DSM-III diagnosis. One's own expert should be warned in advance if the attorney anticipates using the DSM-III on direct examination. During direct examination, the expert's opinion can be substantially enhanced by having the witness detail the diagnostic criteria and how they apply to the person diagnosed, and then by detailing how the differential diagnoses were ruled out. I have found this to be an extremely effective technique, but the expert must have ample time to prepare for such testimony (in practice, the diagnosis frequently is made without direct reference to the specific criteria listed in the book).

The opposing party's expert is not likely to anticipate cross-examination based upon the DSM-III and, therefore, is likely to be vulnerable to impeachment. The attorney should ask the expert whether the numbered diagnosis refers to the DSM-III. If so, the expert should be asked to state what the diagnostic criteria are and how they were applied to the person evaluated. Finally, the expert should be asked whether an analysis of the differential diagnoses was made and, if so, why each such alternative was ruled out. I have found often that witnesses have not considered the differential diagnoses and have not explored the facts which would shed light on their appropriateness.

Where the witness clearly would be able to respond adequately to such cross-examination, the attorney should not attempt it unless his or her expert will be able to offer a more persuasive diagnosis. In addition to the specific disorders listed, the DSM-III sets forth five "axes" upon which the individual is to be evaluated.[35] Therefore, the expert should be prepared to testify concerning all relevant axes. An expert who has used the DSM-III without using it fully is not entitled to the same credibility as one who has followed it completely.

Child Abuse Treatises

Where use of treatises is permitted, child abuse treatises can be very helpful, especially when used with social workers. One of the seminal works in the field is *The Battered Child*,[36] by pediatricians Ray E. Helfer and C. Henry Kempe, who coined the term "battered child syndrome." Those authors later edited *Helping the Battered Child and His Family*,[37] a book every attorney involved in child abuse cases should own. It is considered to be *the* standard work in the area. I have been able to establish through expert testimony that any witness who has not read that book, or at the very least heard of it, is not an expert in the field of child abuse.

This section will discuss the use of treatises with social workers; however, the discussion is equally applicable to physicians, psychologists and other professionals. Because judges frequently undervalue the training and expertise of social workers, use of a child abuse treatise can go far towards strengthening the testimony of a social worker. For example, there are two tables in the book *Helping the Battered Child and His Family*, which provide a checklist for diagnosing physical abuse[38] and for determining whether the home is safe.[39] The social worker should be prepared in advance to go through the various factors and apply them to the case at hand. By demonstrating point by point the analysis of the case, as bolstered by an authoritative treatise, the attorney can greatly enhance the thoroughness of the social worker's evaluation and reliability of his or her conclusions. During direct examination, the social worker should establish the authoritativeness of the book and then testify about the facts and circumstances of the case which apply to each factor. Sometimes the social worker has actually used the book to prepare the case. If the witness has relied on the book, he or she may be cross-examined concerning the book in almost all jurisdictions. If local law does not permit the use of treatises on direct examination, there may be another attorney who is able to use the treatise during cross-examination.[40]

Often social workers have not done a thorough investigation. Almost all of them would concede the authoritativeness of *Helping the Battered Child and His Family,* and the attorney can ask whether the witness assessed the case according to the various guidelines. However, unless the attorney knows in advance that the witness will be unable to apply the factors listed in the two tables mentioned, it is very risky to ask the witness to make an on-the-spot evaluation of whether or not the factors apply. If the witness is able to give that kind of analysis, the effects can be devastating.

In addition to using child abuse treatises during testimony, it is also helpful to use them during the expert's preparation. For example, there is an excellent article which outlines four circumstances of abuse.[41] The author states

> As I see it, there are at least four different sets of circumstances which may lead to a child being seriously neglected, rejected or abused: first, there is the isolated incident which is unlikely to be repeated; second, where one child in the family becomes a "scapegoat"; third, where parents are markedly inadequate; and fourth, where violence is part and parcel of the parental life-style. Each of these circumstances requires, in my view, different treatment, both of the parents and of the child.[42]

The article outlines the differing prognoses for each set of circumstances. I have shown this article to a number of experts during trial preparation and asked them if they agreed with it.

Because they all did, I asked them to analyze the case at hand in terms of the categories, likelihood of repetition of the abuse or neglect and necessary intervention and remedial assistance available. This analysis has proved helpful, whether or not I eventually used the article during trial (which I have on several occasions).

FOOTNOTES

1. See Melvin G. Goldzband, *Custody Cases and Expert Witnesses: A Manual for Attorneys,* Law & Business, Inc., New York: 1980, p. 11.

2. Fed. R. Evid. 615, which has been followed in many state evidence codes, provides that "a person whose presence is shown by a party to be essential to the presentation of his cause" may not be excluded during the testimony of other witnesses.

3. For further discussions of how to testify, see Melvin G. Goldzband, *supra* note 1.

4. For a further discussion on preparing the witness, see Richard A. Givens, *Advocacy: The Art of Pleading a Cause,* Shepard's/McGraw-Hill, Colorado Springs, CO.: 1985.

5. See I. Goldstein and F. Lane, *Goldstein Trial Technique* (2nd ed.), Callaghan, IL.: 1969, section 14.19; and Melvin G. Goldzband, *supra* note 1, p. 29.

6. See Fed. R. Evid. 703 and the state rules patterned after it.

7. See Fed. R. Evid. 705 and the state rules patterned after it.

8. Id.

9. This was admissible under the state of mind exception to the hearsay rule. See Fed. R. Evid. 803(3) and the state rules patterned after it.

10. See, e.g., I. Goldstein and F. Lane, 19.06-19.40, *supra,* note 5; and Jeffrey L. Kestler, *Questioning Techniques and Tactics,* Shepard's/McGraw-Hill, Colorado Springs, CO.: 1982.

11. See, e.g., Melvin G. Goldzband, *supra* note 1, pp. 36-40; P. Fernald, "Puncturing the Pretensions of a Psychiatric Witness," *Family Advocate,* Summer 1980, p. 18; and M. Inker, *More Tips on Cross-Examining Experts,* id. at p. 20.

12. S. Hathaway and J. McKinley, *Minnesota Multiphasic Personality Inventory,* 1943. This is a multiple choice test, consisting of 550 questions to which the patient must answer yes or no. The results of the test are plotted on a graph which is then analyzed.

13. The test has also been standardized a number of times with normal populations.

14. For one criticism of the standardization of the MMPI, see, e.g., A. Gilliland and R. Colgin, "Norms Reliability, and Forms of the MMPI," *Journal of Consulting Psychology* 15:435, 1951.

15. D. Weschler, *Weschler Adult Intelligence Scale,* 1968. A newly revised test is available. See D. Weschler, *Weschler Adult Intelligence Scale—Revised,* 1981. A Spanish language test, standardized in Puerto Rico, is also available. See D. Weschler, *Escala de Inteligencia Weschler para Adultos,* (R. Green and J. Martinez, trans. 1965).

16. D. Weschler, *Weschler Intelligence Scale for Children—Revised,* 1974. This test is used for children between 6 and 16. For children between 4 an 6½, see, D. Weschler, *Weschler Preschool and Primary Scale of Intelligence,* 1967. For children between the ages 3 to 30 months, see P. Cattell, *Cattell Infant Intelligence Scale,* 1960.

17. Hermann Rorschach, *Psychodiagnostik,* 1932. In this test, the patient is shown a series of cards of inkblots. The patient describes what he or she sees in the picture, often giving several answers.

18. Henry A. Murray and Leopold Bellak, *Thematic Apperception Test,* 1973.

19. Leopold Bellak and S. Bellak, *Children's Apperception Test,* 1974.

20. See Fed. R. Evid. 702 and the state rules patterned after it.

21. An interesting study asked various categories of people to define whether certain behavior constituted abuse and to rank how serious different abusive behavior was. The wide variety of responses was instructive. See, Jeanne M. Giovannoni and Rosina Becerra, *Defining Child Abuse,* Free Press, New York: 1979.

22. The Supreme Court of Alaska decided an interesting custody case which points out the importance of not using dominant culture biases to deprive a minority culture father (in that case, an Eskimo) living according to his culture's norms, of custody in *Carle v. Carle,* 503 P.2d 1050·(Alaska 1972).

23. The phrase was first coined by Dr. C. Henry Kempe in 1961. Since that time, courts have accepted testimony of the syndrome by physicians. See, e.g., *People v. Jackson,* 18 Cal. App.3d 504, 95 Cal. Rptr. 919 (1971); *People v. Ellis,* 589 P.2d 494 (Colo. App. 1978); *People v. Platter,* 89 Ill. App.3d 803, 45 Ill. Dec. 48, 412 N.E.2d 181 (1980); *James v. State,* 5 Md. App. 647, 248 A.2d 910 (1969); *Schleret v. State,* 311 N.W.2d 843 (Minn. 1981); *People v. Henson,* 33 N.Y.2d 63, 349 N.Y.S.2d 657, 304 N.E.2d 358 (1973); *State v. Mulder,* 29 Wash. App. 513, 629 P.2d 462 (1981); But see, *State v. Loebach,* 310 N.W.2d 58 (Minn. 1981) (admissible only if defendant puts his character in evidence).

24. Fed. R. Evid. 705, after which many state evidence are patterned, provides that the expert may be required to disclose the underlying facts or data upon which his or her opinion is based. Fed. R. Evid. 703 provides that those facts or data need not be independently admissible in evidence. Therefore, otherwise inadmissible evidence may be admitted on cross-examination by way of inquiry into the basis of the opinion expressed.

25. See, generally, 6 Wigmore: *Evidence,* Sections 1690-1708 (Chadbourn rev. 1970); 29 Am. Jur.2d *Evidence,* Sections 888-890; 84 A.L.R.2d 1338, and the cases cited therein.

26. See, 60 A.L.R.2d 77 and the cases cited therein.

27. See cases cited in 60 A.L.R.2d 77, 81-87; *State v. Galloway,* 275 N.W.2d 736 (Iowa 1979).

28. See cases cited at 60 A.L.R.2d 77 at 87-93.

29. See cases cited at 60 A.L.R.2d 77 at 94-98; *Gaston v. Hunter,* 121 Ariz. 33, 588 P.2d 326 (Ariz. App. 1978); *Mark v. Colgate University,* 53 A.D.2d 884, 385 N.Y.S.2d 621, (1976); *Guidry v. Phillips,* 580 S.W.2d 883 (Tex. Civ. App. 14th Dist. 1979); *McComish v. De Soi,* 42 N.J. 274, 200 A.2d 116 (1964).

30. See cases cited at 60 A.L.R.2d 77, at 98-104; *Ravenis v. Detroit General Hospital,* 63 Mich. App. 79, 234 N.W.2d 411 (1975).

31. See, e.g. *Reilly v. Pinkus,* 338 U.S. 269, 70 S.Ct. 110, 94 L.Ed. 63 (1949); *Darling v. Charleston Community Memorial Hospital,* 33 Ill.2d 326, 211 N.E.2d 253 (1965), *cert. den.* 383 U.S. 946, 16 L.Ed.2d 209, 86 S.Ct. 1204 (1966); *Dabroe v. Rhodes Co.,* 64 Wash.2d 431, 392 P.2d 317 (1964).

32. Such as age at onset, sex ratio and prevalence, course, impairment, complications, familial pattern and differential diagnosis.

33. American Psychiatric Association, *Diagnostic and Statistical Manual of Mental Disorders,* 55 (3rd ed.), 1980.

34. Id.

35. Basically, clinical syndromes (Axis I), personality disorders and specific developmental disorders (Axis II), physical disorders and conditions (Axis III), severity of psychosocial stressors (Axis IV) and highest level of adaptive functioning past year (Axis V).

36. Ray E. Helfer and C. Henry Kempe, *The Battered Child* (1st ed.), University of Chicago Press, Chicago: 1968. (The fourth edition is scheduled for publication in 1987).

37. C. Henry Kempe and Ray E. Helfer, *Helping the Battered Child and His Family,* J.B. Lippincott Company, Philadelphia: 1972.

38. Id. at 73.

39. Id. at 78.

40. For example, in many child protective services cases the state's attorney and child's attorney have a similar interest in showing the abuse,

and they can agree in advance to have the one doing the cross-examination use treatises.

41. M. Pringle, "The Needs of Children," in *The Maltreatment of Children,* Selwyn Smith (ed.), Professional Education, Chicago: 1978, p. 221.

42. Id. at 234.

THE GUARDIAN *AD LITEM* IN DIVORCE CASES

Carol Higley Lane, Esq.

The concept of independent representation of children springs generally from the Fourteenth Amendment of the United States Constitution. The due process clause entitles a person to a fair and impartial trial before an impartial tribunal in both civil and criminal cases.[1] The neutrality requirement helps to guarantee that life, liberty and/or property will not be taken on the basis of an erroneous or distorted conception of facts or law.[2] At the same time, it preserves both the appearance and reality of fairness, "generating the feeling, so important to popular government, that justice has been done."[3]

INDEPENDENT REPRESENTATION OF CHILDREN

In the United States Supreme Court

The Supreme Court has recognized that the protections of the Fourteenth Amendment are not for adults alone.[4] A

Reprinted with portions revised to lend a broader application from the *Advanced Family Law Course Book,* © August 1980, State Bar of Texas.

number of Supreme Court decisions have recognized and upheld the liberty interests of children against infringement by state action.[5]

Independent representation of children in any family law proceeding was rare prior to *In re Gault*,[6] in 1967. *Gault* dealt with the complete absence of due process in a juvenile court proceeding held to declare a minor "delinquent" and incarcerate him for his act. One of the fundamental rights found to have been denied in *Gault* was the right to counsel at every stage of juvenile court delinquency proceedings. Even though *Gault* was decided in the context of delinquency matters, this case is the starting point in arguing for a child's right to independent representation before the courts.

A more recent case, *Stanley v. Illinois*,[7] dealt with the absence of due process in a proceeding to terminate the parental rights of a natural father to his children. The court in *Stanley*, in speaking of the liberty interests of families, stated that not only parents, but also their children, have justiciable constitutional rights that may be pursued by law.[8] Several Supreme Court Justices have posited the proposition that children are entitled to *more* protection than adults, since childhood is a particularly vulnerable time of life.[9] In 1962 prior to *Gault*, Mr. Justice Black observed that, in cases where the child's custody is at issue, the custody decision cannot be left to the parents to decide, especially where emotion and prejudice cloud parental judgment.[10]

To date no United States Supreme Court decision has dealt expressly with a child's right to representation in divorce cases. The court has decided those issues known as "children's rights" on a case-by-case basis and has not, to date, elevated the status of childhood to a "suspect" classification (unlike race, religion, national origin or alienage) to determine deprivation of rights under the Fourteenth Amendment. The Court has shown a preference for determining children's issues within the context of family rights and privacy found in *Griswold v. Connecticut*[11] and its progeny, or, *Meyer v.*

Nebraska[12] and *Pierce v. Society of Sisters*,[13] and the cases following them.

In the Lower Federal Courts

A few federal district courts have ventured into the area of legal representation of children in divorce custody matters. The Federal Rules of Civil Procedure may be used to grant standing to a child to file a petition in federal court, challenging the constitutionality of a custody determination in state court, made either contrary to the child's wishes or without any solicitation of the child's desires.[14] Even if a child is granted standing, however, and *arguendo*, a case or controversy is found to exist, this does not necessarily mean that the child's interests will be vindicated.

In *Salaices v. Sabraw*,[15] three children sued to enjoin enforcement of a visitation order, alleging a violation of due process. In denying their claim the court noted that if due process had been violated, it was minimal, since the state court judge heard the children's objection to visitation through their counsel, a social worker and the children themselves. The court further noted that visitation was not the same as custody and distinguished another federal district court case in which the court had been sympathetic to the child's custody claim.[16]

In *Goldsmith v. Jekanowski*[17] the child was challenging a custody order wherein a state court had ordered her custody without consideration of the child's wishes. The minor child, through her retained counsel, asserted a right to participate in the decision-making process concerning her placement under the due process clause of the Fourteenth Amendment, which the federal court sustained. More recently, in *Bergstrom v. Bergstrom*,[18] a child, through her guardian *ad litem*, sued her parents to restrain her mother from carrying out the order of the Superior Court for the District of Columbia, which required that the child, a U.S. citizen, be returned to Norway, which was the home of the mother. The Bergstrom Court sustained the child's plea, asserting that as a citizen of the United States, even though a minor child, she had an inalienable right to the privileges of U.S. citizenship fundamental to her well-being. Observing that there were no treaties between the United States and Norway extending the privileges of U.S. citizenship to U.S. citizens residing in Norway (or in Behrain on the Persian Gulf, where it appeared that the mother was headed), the court stated, "This court has been shown no laws, statutes or holdings which would authorize a court of domestic relations to remove a minor American citizen from the protection of the Constitution and the laws of the United States against her will."[19]

In Other States

Wisconsin and New Hampshire mandate the appointment of a guardian *ad litem* in all divorce-related custody disputes.[20] Michigan allows a public prosecutor to intervene in divorce custody disputes on behalf of the child, if it is in the child's interest to do so.[21] The Uniform Marriage and Divorce Act, codified in some states, gives courts discretion to appoint an attorney to represent children.[22] Some states have adopted a policy of appointing attorneys for children, although their states' statutory language is couched in permissive terms.[23] The majority of states leave representation of the children of divorce to trial court discretion and do not recognize a due process right to representation for these children.[24]

No state considers legal representation of children in divorce cases where custody is not contested. Thus, since approximately 90 percent of divorce cases are uncontested, the custody wishes of the vast majority of children of divorce are ignored. One case has been found where a state court removed custody of a minor from her parents on the initiative of the child. *In re Snyder*, involved a child who threatened to run away from home unless the court took action on her behalf.

The Court in its *parens patriae* role granted the child's request. In effect, the child in *Snyder* was divorcing her parents![25]

THE LAY GUARDIAN *AD LITEM*

Because of the failure of the legal system to recognize the needs of children to be represented in all cases in which their interests are involved, there is a trend in a number of jurisdictions to establish child advocacy groups composed of lay persons who will serve as representatives of children in court and administrative hearings.[26] Some of these persons are volunteers and some are paid social workers who are permitted to appear in court in some states. The majority of states require lawyers to represent children before their courts.[27]

Advantages

Lay guardians, especially volunteers, are usually less expensive than lawyers. They may have more time and ability to investigate than attorneys. Professionals from the behavioral or social sciences who act as lay guardians *ad litem* usually have more knowledge of child development, and social and psychological issues than lawyers have. Lay guardians, often highly motivated, are more likely to continue to represent the child after formal court proceedings are completed, thus providing expertise for the court should custody or related issues decided by the court need to be modified at a later date.

Disadvantages

The primary disadvantage of lay guardians is their lack of legal training when attempting to represent children in court or at administrative hearings. A lay guardian would still need to retain counsel for the child, thus introducing another person into the proceedings.

THE ATTORNEY-GUARDIAN *AD LITEM*

The general trend since *Gault, supra,* has been in the direction of recognition of children as persons with justiciable interests which can best be protected in an adversary hearing. Federal statute mandates the appointment of a guardian *ad litem* (who need not be an attorney) in all child abuse and neglect cases, in order to receive federal aid in this area.[28] Since a majority of the states require attorneys to fill this function by law, there is a growing need for a sophisticated child advocacy bar, specially trained with the unique skills that legal representation of children requires in the behavioral and social sciences.

Advantages

Competent legal representation helps to insure that judges will receive all available information relevant to the jurisdictional and dispositional decision-making process. A skilled attorney will be much better equipped to handle the procedural and substantive details of pretrial discovery and courtroom representation. A lawyer can better prepare the child's own case, present evidence beneficial to the child, exclude evidence harmful to the child, examine and cross-examine witnesses, make legal arguments to the court and appeal the decision, if necessary.

Disadvantages

Lawyers are usually very expensive. Thorough preparation for representation of a child takes a great deal of time which attorneys may be unwilling or unable to spare, particularly if they must accept small or no remuneration for this work.

Attorneys generally do not have the behavioral expertise needed to conduct the investigation so necessary for this type of representation. Because fees for representing children tend to be low, usually only inexperienced, newly licensed attorneys are willing to accept minors as clients, both for the courtroom experience and to help pay law office overhead until better paying clients materialize.

CURRENT METHODS OF *AD LITEM* SELECTION

One method of solving the problems with both lay guardians and attorney guardians is to appoint both types to represent each child. Another method is to provide attorneys with the professional assistance needed to adequately investigate the case and provide recommendations for treatment. Both of these methods are unlikely to find favor in the majority of jurisdictions since they are doubly costly propositions.

In some locales public defenders or legal aid societies have attempted to form a core group of *ad litems* for children from among their ranks; however, this method of providing representation may create a conflict of interest if these organizations also represent parents or the state.

Additionally, these organizations typically are too overwhelmed by their case loads to take on the duties required of an effective *ad litem*. Also their attorneys are usually poorly paid, relative to the rest of the legal profession, and those that might represent children are likely to be the most inexperienced in the group, without expertise in child development or psychology.

Some jurisdictions appoint private practitioners to represent children. In some instances, the practitioner's name is drawn at random, either from the roster of the entire local bar, or from the group of family law practitioners in the community. Unfortunately these attorneys usually do not have expertise in representing children. They have neither the time nor the inclination to do the proper investigation because they are "waste time" on preparing a case for a minor client. The trend toward requiring a certain number of *pro bono publico* hours of legal service from every member of the legal profession each year has been suggested in relation to legal representation of children. No reference as to the methods of training attorneys to provide adequate representation in this area has been made to date. One can speculate that this method of providing legal services for children will be as unsatisfactory as drawing names from the roster of the entire local bar.

Another trend is to appoint law students as *ad litems* for children in court. Usually students are motivated to do a thorough investigation, if properly supervised; however, they are inexperienced in courtroom legal techniques.

Many judges appoint *ad litems* from among their attorney friends, taxing the parties with heavy legal fees as costs to insure that these attorneys will be paid. The large fee insures that these attorneys will continue to serve in this capacity. Unfortunately this method of securing representation of children often smacks of patronage, without consideration of the skills needed to truly represent children.

Some courts, over a period of time, develop their own resource pool of attorneys with expertise in the areas of behavioral science and child development. While this approach appears to be the best, in so far as obtaining quality of representation is concerned, unless payment for services of these expert attorneys *ad litem* is insured, these *ad litems* will be forced by economic necessity to move into more remunerative areas of law.

ROLE OF THE APPOINTED ATTORNEY-GUARDIAN *AD LITEM*

The attorney *ad litem's* role in representing children, in addition to being that of an advocate for the child, must also be a composite of the specialized skills of mediator, counselor and investigator.

The earlier the attorney is appointed in a contested custody case, the more effectively he can perform his tasks. Appointment should be made as soon as a real custody dispute is evident. Upon appointment the *ad litem* must examine the court file for its contents. He should determine whether a social worker has been assigned to investigate. If that has not been done, a motion requesting a social evaluation should be made. Although the social worker's opinion is not determinative, it may aid the attorney's investigation.

The *ad litem* must also file an answer for the child as well as a motion for costs. Additional motions for costs may be introduced throughout the proceedings, as needed, to cover the *ad litem's* expense of discovery.

Contact with the attorneys for both parties must be made as soon after appointment as possible, explaining that the *ad litem* represents *only* the child. Seek their permission to interview the parties. It is important to secure the cooperation of these attorneys. The lawyer for a party will usually have a view of the *ad litem* that reflects the strength or weakness of his client's case. Try to explain the *ad litem's* role as one that frees the attorneys for the parents to give their undivided loyalty to their clients. Do not have any *ex parte* conversations with the judge hearing the case. This will destroy any trust or respect of the *ad litem* with the parties or their attorneys.

If the trial court wants a written investigative report from the *ad litem*, with a written recommendation as to the custody of the child, be sure that the parties and their attorneys are cognizant of this at the outset. If possible, get the parties to stipulate the admissibility of this report as an exception to hearsay coming from an expert. If used by the court, the report should be reasonably available to the parties prior to trial and made part of the record. If a report is submitted, be sure it reflects the child's desires since the *ad litem* is speaking for that child. Even if the *ad litem* is not convinced that the child's wishes are in the child's best interests, the child's preferences and the reasons for them should be stated. The attorney should be very wary of opposing the child's preference. There may be very good reasons for this preference that he cannot readily articulate and that are not easily observable.

Advocacy Preparation

The attorney should exercise independent judgment and not rely on reports from investigative agencies or experts. During investigation the attorney should act to enhance the parent–child relationship and avoid inflicting needless harm and expense.

Always visit several times with the children involved in the case. Often even very young children have definite viewpoints and preferences that, once they know and trust an adult, they readily share. Even with an infant or very young child, an observant *ad litem* can pick up behavioral clues that may indicate a preference for one parent or the other. Older children are usually delighted to have their own legal counsel. Often they have been wishing for someone to explain what will happen to them, someone in whom they can confide their feelings about their parents' divorce. The minor client should have the legal process explained to him. He should also know that, although the *ad litem* will probably be talking about him in court, things told to the *ad litem* by the child are confidential and will not be revealed to his parents or their attorneys unless he allows the *ad litem* to do so. Informality and friendliness are necessary ingredients in interviewing children. The *ad litem* should endeavor to conduct any interviews with the child in the child's familiar environment. If the child does not want to participate in the investigatory process, he should not be forced to do so. However, do not shut off lines of communication with the child. He may just be shy or frightened and may want to talk with his attorney later. If the parents' attorneys wish to interview the child, they must seek permission from the *ad litem* to do so. All child interviews with attorneys for the parents must be conducted in the presence of the *ad litem*.

If the parents' attorneys are cooperative, the *ad litem* may obtain pertinent records concerning the child through them. If they refuse to cooperate, the *ad litem* must not hesitate to file motions to subpoena records concerning the child's welfare.

Interviews must be held with the child's teacher, minister, physicians, friends and close relatives. Except when a child is emotionally disturbed or if the child is noncommunicative, professional evaluations of the child should *not* be sought when other persons can guide the attorney. Psychiatric evaluation of a child under the age of three years is usually a waste of time and money; however, developmental evaluations can be valuable, especially if the child is observed before and after changes of placement. On the other hand, evaluations merely for the purpose of divorce trials lead to swearing matches in court. Only if the child has been receiving counseling or therapy on an ongoing basis is it worthwhile to obtain an evaluation from that counselor or therapist. Usually the child's pediatrician is a much better source of information (and a much better witness) than a psychiatrist. If a psychological or psychiatric evaluation is absolutely necessary, the *ad litem* should choose the expert, giving preference to one who will be able to give continuing therapeutic assistance to the child and his family. The expert should be instructed to give information, not just conclusions, in his report.

If an investigation by a social worker from a service agency has been ordered, generally the worker will prepare a written report. The *ad litem* should meet with the social worker, coordinating the two investigatory efforts to avoid duplication. The *ad litem* should ascertain the contents of the social report. The social worker's evaluation may be contrary to the child's wishes and the *ad litem's* perceptions of the case.

If the attorney *ad litem* cannot settle the case, and if delay will not serve his own trial strategy, the attorney must press to have the custody issues heard quickly, filing a motion to sever the custody issues from the rest of the divorce proceedings in the interest of the child.

If the custody dispute is one that has arisen after the divorce has been granted, where the noncustodial party alleges grounds for a change in custody, the attorney *ad litem* must ascertain if there really are sufficient grounds to change custody. If the *ad litem,* as a neutral fact-gatherer, believes that the moving party will not sustain the burden of proof necessary to secure custody of the child, and if change in custody is not in the child's best interest, he should tell the movant's attorney of his view. Never spring surprise recommendations regarding custody on the attorneys during or at the end of trial. Because the *ad litem,* as mediator, can often impel settlement, it behooves him to move toward out-of-court dispute resolution in the best interests of his client.

Formal Discovery

If the attorney for the parties are unwilling to allow the *ad litem* to talk to the parties, the *ad litem* must file interrogatories, seeking detailed information, for example:

- A party's employment record
- Economic status
- Physical and mental health (past and present)
- Education
- Organizational affiliations
- Home environment
- Plans to care for and educate the child
- Insurance benefits
- Names of persons treating the party for mental or physical illness, type of treatment, kind of disease, and prognosis
- Any personal knowledge concerning the child's health from the physician(s), teachers, and other persons close to the child
- Any personal knowledge concerning the child's expressed or implied preference for managing conservator
- Why custody should lie with that party and,
- Any letters, recordings or transcripts of conversations between that party and the opposing party.

The *ad litem* must be notified by counsel for the parties of taking of any depositions. He must be present when depositions are taken. He must participate in the questioning of the parties. The *ad litem* can also arrange to take depositions on his own with notice to the attorneys for all parties.

If problems arise during the discovery period, try to meet with the attorneys for both parties together to work out a solution. If the other attorneys and their clients are uncooperative during this period, and if a serious problem develops either in seeking discoverable materials or with the child in his relationship with his parents, the *ad litem* should file a motion stating the problem and seek a hearing date to air the grievance before the court. A court hearing with all parties present will make everyone aware of the problem, and all will be present to explain the reasons for the problem and to hear the court's response.

If psychiatric examination is essential, ask the court to order it for all parties and all children whose custody is at issue. Frame the motion to request that the physician who sees the parties and children will see the parents alone, together, with and without the children, and will see the children alone and together too.

If unable to secure a settlement prior to trial, file a motion to have the child visit with the judge in his chambers to state his preference. After the child's visit, ask for a pretrial conference of all counsel and the judge, in a last effort to effectuate settlement.

Trial

Assume that the trial will be to a jury and plan accordingly. File and get a hearing on motion(s) *in limine* in an effort to suppress evidence that may be prejudicial to the child's interests and which is likely to taint the judge and jury.

Issue subpoenas for witnesses to appear and testify on behalf of the child. Be sure to prepare these witnesses concerning courtroom procedure, demeanor or attire and the types of questions that will likely be asked. Prepare them for cross-examination by attorneys for the parties.

Create a trial notebook containing relevant statutes, rules and case law support. Inventory documents to be submitted as evidence. Prepare questions to ask each witness.

Request the permission to *voir dire* the jury panel. It is discretionary with the trial court to allow the *ad litem* to conduct *voir dire* and make preemptory strikes. Be sure to question witnesses called on behalf of both parties. Present witnesses on behalf of the child.

Pediatrician.   This physician usually makes a fine witness simply because he is more believable than a psychiatrist. The jury can more readily identify with him from their common experiences with pediatricians or family doctors.

Psychologist.   It has been held in custody modification hearings that a psychologist's testimony, after the psychologist had evaluated and counseled the children as to their welfare and their post-divorce environment, was admissible evidence.

Children.   State statutes vary as to when a child is presumed to be competent. If the judge refuses to allow the child to testify, in order to preserve error for appeal, the *ad litem* must object and dictate into the record what the child would have testified to if allowed to do so.

Remember that the trial court has discretion to disregard the preference of a minor, regardless of age, if the court believes the child's best interests are better served with custodial arrangements other than those the child desires.

Social Worker.   If the social worker's report has been submitted to the court and made part of the record, it is a good idea to have the worker present in court to testify. If the worker's view supports the *ad litem* and the child, in-court testimony by the worker takes care of hearsay problems. If the worker's report is contrary to the child's wishes and/or the *ad litem's* investigative discoveries, the worker should be questioned carefully on the reasons for his conclusions and, if possible, his report should be discredited. An *ex parte* social report submitted to a judge carries enormous impact and may outweigh the testimony of the parties, the child and other witnesses in influencing the trial court's decision.

Guardian ad Litem. It is not essential that the guardian *ad litem* testify concerning his services as long as there is some evidence to support the fee awarded him by the court. Since the *ad litem* is an officer of the court, the judge has broad discretion in setting his fees. The trial court's determination of reasonable fees will not be overturned unless there is a clear abuse of discretion apparent from the record. Fees for the guardian *ad litem* are to be taxed as costs against the parties.

Close of Trial

Summation. The attorney *ad litem* should always make a recommendation to the court in regard to the custody of his client; however, even if the *ad litem* does not make a specific recommendation in this regard, the trial court still has the power and responsibility to base its decision on the best interest of the child.

Judgment. The attorney *ad litem* should ask to help prepare the portion of the decree dealing with conservatorship. Be specific when setting visitation terms. Give the possessory conservator the same rights as the managing conservator in providing medical treatment for the child during periods of visitation.

Review the terms of conservatorship with the parties and their attorneys, as well as the child, so that all understand them.

Motion for New Trial. Technical rules of pleading and practice are of little importance when determining issues involving the best interest of the child. Ordinary rules restricting the granting of a new trial for newly discovered evidence are not to be applied rigidly in child custody cases. This does not mean that the trial court should grant a new trial on the basis of "new" evidence that is merely cumulative or inadmissible. However, if strong new evidence concerning the best interests of the children is presented to the court after determination of custody is made, failure to grant a new trial may be an abuse of discretion, since the protection of the child is the paramount concern in custody suits. Although inexperience or mistake of one's attorney is ordinarily not grounds for a new trial (since the children, not the parents, are the real parties in interest), the court's primary responsibility is to protect the children unrestrained by technical rules.

CONCLUSION

Despite the increased national attention to the rights of children, it is likely that children will continue to be denied their due process right to full legal representation in many proceedings where their interests are at risk. Continued use of the best interest doctrine in the majority of United States jurisdictions promotes the denial of a child's due process right because the best interest standard is incapable of precise definition and subject to broad judicial discretion.[29] Commentators have questioned whether the rule's intent is effectively being met.[30]

The reluctance of the judiciary to acknowledge the important research of social and behavioral scientists in areas of human growth and development, particularly in regard to the concept of psychological parenting, demonstrates the validity of the commentator's query. This concept's partial implementation would require entering more permanent custody decisions, subject to reappraisal only under very compelling circumstances. Psychological parenting suggests that custody disputes be settled rapidly, when they arise so that a child won't have to wait to have his future determined when the divorce case is heard on the merits. It would be preferable to have custody issues determined at a hearing held only for that purpose shortly after the divorce action is filed. The concept of psychological parenting also urges courts to give heavy weight to the child's preference, which can be ascertained only if the child is given full party status in custody disputes. Full party status requires that the child be given competent legal counsel to represent him on all issues surrounding the child's future development.

Child advocacy, as a specialized area of legal practice within family law, must be accorded status within the legal profession on par with other areas of legal specialization. The bar must be made to recognize its grave responsibility to train attorneys to represent children, promoting this area of legal practice as one worthy of pursuit and urging the provision of financial resources to provide adequate compensation for such attorneys. Children are the future of our country. They are the judges of our civilization. The legal profession is the one most identifiable group in control of our nation's destiny. It must lead the way in providing for the needs of helpless children whose lives are tangled in the law.

FOOTNOTES

1. *Carey v. Piphus*, 435 U.S. 247, 259-62 (1978).

2. *Mathews v. Eldridge*, 424 U.S. 319, 344 (1976).

3. *Joint Anti-Fascist Committee v. McGrath*, 341 U.S. 123, 162 (1951) (Frankfurter, J., concurring).

4. *Carey v. Population Services Int'l*, 431 U.S. 678, 692 (1977). See, e.g. *Planned Parenthood of Central Mo v. Danforth*, 428 U.S. 52, 74 (1976); *Tinker v. Des Moines Independent Community School Dist.*, 393 U.S. 503, 511 (1969); *In re Gault*, 387 U.S. 1 (1967).

5. *Planned Parenthood of Central Mo, supra* (privacy); *Goss v. Lopez,* 419 U.S. 565 (1975) (while upholding school suspension, recognizing children's right to have access to benefits created by state law), *Tinker, supra* (speech); *Gault, supra* (liberty); *Ingraham v. Wright,* 430 U.S. 651 (1977) (right of security of the person, recognized but not applied to this case).

6. 387 U.S. 1 (1967).

7. 405 U.S. 645 (1972).

8. See, e.g., *Prince v. Massachusetts,* 321 U.S. 158, 165 (1944).

9. See, e.g., *Parham v. J.R.,* 422 U.S. 584, 625 (1979) (Brennan, J., concurring in part and dissenting in part). See also, *Wisconsin v. Yoder,* 406 U.S. 205, 242 (1972) (Douglas, J., dissenting); *San Antonio Independent School Dist. v. Rodriguez,* 411 U.S. 1, 70 (1973) (Marshall, J., dissenting) (arguments for the status of childhood to trigger closer scrutiny for purposes of Fourteenth Amendment analysis).

10. *Ford v. Ford,* 371 U.S. 187, 193 (1962).

11. 381 U.S. 479 (1965).

12. 262 U.S. 390 (1923).

13. 268 U.S. 510 (1924).

14. See, Fed. R. Civ. P. rules 19(a) and (b); 24(a)(2).

15. 400 F.Supp. 367 (ND Cal 1975).

16. *Goldsmith v. Jekanowski,* Civ. No. 75-1308F (D Mass. April 28, 1975) (Memorandum and Injunctive Order).

17. Id.

18. 478 F.Supp 434 (D. N. D. 1979).

19. Id. at 440.

20. Supreme Court Order, 50 Wis.2d ix (1971), creating Wis. Stat. Ann. section 767.045 (1981) with *deMontigny v. deMontigny,* 75 Wis.2d 131, 233 N.W.2d 463 (1975); N.H. Rev. Stat. Ann. 458:17-a (1985).

21. Mich. Comp. Laws Ann. section 552.45 (1967).

22. Uniform Marriage and Divorce Act section 310.

23. Examples include: Conn. Gen Stat. Ann. section 46b-54 (Supp. 1986); D.C. Code Encycl. section 16-918 (1967); Iowa Code Ann. section 598.12 (1981); Mont. Rev. Code Ann. section 40-4-205 (1985); Neb. Rev. Stat. section 42-358(1) (1984); Or. Rev. Stat. section 107.425(3) (1984); Utah Code Ann. section 30-3-11.2 (1984); Wash. Rev. Code Ann. section 26.09.110 (1982).

24. See, e.g. *Leigh v. Aiken,* 311 So.2d 444 (Ala Ct App 1975).

25. *In re Snyder,* 85 Wash.2d 182, 532 P.2d 278 (1975).

26. See, e.g., J. S. Wallerstein and J. B. Kelly, "Divorce Counselling: A Community Service for Families in the Midst of Divorce," *American Journal of Orthopsychiatry* 47:4, 1977.

27. See, e.g., "Uniform Marriage and Divorce Act, Section 310 Comment," *Family Law Quarterly* 5:205, 235, 1971.

28. 42 U.S.C. section 5103(b)(2)(G)(1974).

29. See, e.g., B. N. Henszey, "Visitation by a Non-custodial Parent: What is the 'Best Interests' Doctrine?", *Journal of Family Law* 15:213, 225, 1977.

30. See, e.g., Comment, "The Rights of Children: A Trust Model," *Fordham Law Review* 46:669, 742, 1978.

PROFESSIONAL AND AGENCY LIABILITY FOR NEGLIGENCE IN CHILD PROTECTION†

Donald C. Bross, J.D., Ph.D.

Child protection has become a multidisciplinary field and, therefore, social workers, doctors, police officers and mental health professionals have been held to be negligent in carrying out duties to children. Suits for negligence in the area of child protection have become frequent as the number of reported child abuse and neglect cases has increased.

The diagnostic professions of medicine and mental health are often involved early in child protection proceedings because of legal requirements for diagnosis and reporting. Social workers and police officers have been charged with failure to respond appropriately to reports of child abuse. Cases of inadequate selection of, or monitoring of placements into, foster homes are also associated with social workers. This section will consider these cases and discuss the various defenses raised.

Revised and reprinted with permission from *Law, Medicine and Health Care*, Vol. 11, No. 2; © 1983, American Society of Law and Medicine, Boston, MA.

†For additional citations regarding recent liability cases, refer to the end of this chapter.

FAILURE TO DIAGNOSE

Landeros v. Flood[1] is the leading case on failure to report suspected child abuse and neglect, but the language of the California Supreme Court in this case also makes it clear that the failure to diagnose suspected child abuse and neglect, as with other failures of diagnosis, can provide a basis for malpractice litigation. Although the following principle has not yet been specifically applied to child abuse or neglect, some courts have allowed claims of malpractice in the mental health field for the failure to warn a potential victim of a violent mental patient when, by the reasonable standards of the profession, the mental health professional should have known the patient was likely to harm a potential victim.[2]

FAILURE TO REPORT

The advent of reporting laws in all fifty of the United States[3] has raised the possibility that courts could label failure to report child abuse as negligence per se in malpractice litigation. While some state statutes have created a specific civil liability for failure to report suspected child abuse or neglect,[4] *Landeros v. Flood* was based on a California criminal statute punishing failure to report suspected abuse as a misdemeanor.[5] The California Supreme Court noted that failure to comply with the statute would constitute negligence per se.

The common law basis for a mental health professional's duty to report suspected child abuse can be found in *Tarasoff v. Regents of the University of California.*[6] A University of California psychologist believed that a patient would kill his girlfriend. The psychologist's request to campus police that the patient be detained was overridden by a supervising psychiatrist on the basis of physician–patient confidentiality. After the student killed his girlfriend, her parents brought a wrongful death action, resulting in a $200,000 award upheld by the California Supreme Court. The New Jersey Superior Court adopted the *Tarasoff* principle in *McIntosh v. Milano.*[7] In *Bellah v. Greenson,*[8] the California Court of Appeals limited *Tarasoff* to circumstances where there is a risk of violent assault, as contrasted with a risk of self-inflicted harm or harm to property.

Another case limiting the application of the *Tarasoff* principle is *Shaw v. Glickman,*[9] where the court ruled that there was no duty to warn because of the patient–physician privilege. However, the facts in *Shaw* differ from the *Tarasoff* situation in several respects—most notably in that the therapist was dealing with a group psychotherapy program and that it was, therefore, not as clear that the psychotherapist knew or should have known of the risk to the eventual victim. These cases define the extent of the *Tarasoff* principle and suggest limitations on its application to child abuse situations.

The case of *Florida v. Groff*[10] appears to limit the trend of accountability for failure to report suspected child abuse and neglect. However, the prior Florida statute on child abuse reporting was narrow and only required reports by persons who were directly serving children. Dr. Stephen Groff, a psychiatrist, was treating the father, George Hoover, whom he believed was sexually abusing his daughter; the physician failed to take the steps necessary to protect the child. The criminal charge against Dr. Groff was dropped based on this narrow interpretation of the Florida statute.[11]

Another type of case that may prove pertinent in analyzing a situation of possible failure to report child abuse and neglect is the communicable disease case. Courts have permitted actions against persons mandated to report specified communicable diseases to health officials[12] and against professionals who fail to warn identifiable and foreseeable victims of the possibility of contagion.[13] Several criminal cases for failure to report suspected child abuse and neglect are mentioned later in this article.

FAILURE TO INVESTIGATE REPORT PROPERLY

At least two types of failure are encompassed by this heading. The first is the situation in which a delayed response to a suspected child abuse report has led to a complaint and a civil prosecution. The other type of case under this heading involves overreacting to reports of suspected child abuse or neglect.

In *Mammo v. Arizona*,[14] a noncustodial father visited his two toddler children, but was not allowed by the mother to view his infant child during the visit. The father was concerned about bruises noted on the older children, aged about two and four. He reported these to the Arizona Social Services Department (ASSD), which apparently saw no urgency in the case and believed the matter should be handled by the father's divorce attorney. Ten days later the infant was killed and the father brought a wrongful death action against ASSD for failure to respond to a report.

Negligence per se cases have been filed in other states for failure to respond to a report of child abuse or neglect.[15] One of the cases, settled for $82,500, was filed under the Iowa Tort Claims Act. The plaintiff alleged negligent investigation and supervision, failure to employ qualified employees, failure to staff sufficiently and failure to remove the child from an unsafe home.[16] Several of these claims are discussed below in more detail.

In Florida, the failure of police to follow state statutory and internal departmental procedures led to a suit by a trustee (a bank) on behalf of two abused children.[17] The trustee alleged that the police failed to respond adequately to repeated calls by neighbors who were reporting possible abuse. The dissenting judge criticized the majority's decision for the plaintiff as an unwarranted expansion of exceptions to municipal immunity law in Florida.[18]

The other side of this dilemma can be seen in a Colorado case where the parents of an infant girl alleged defamation against the county as a result of a report of suspected sexual abuse.[19] The county attempted to limit the parents' discovery of departmental records through the confidentiality and immunity clauses of the state reporting statute, but the appellate court directed that the information be provided if certain requirements could be satisfied. In particular, the confidentiality statute required a showing that the county had acted in good faith in order for the immunity clause to apply. The appellate court ruled that the issue of good faith had been properly raised, and that the county had not sufficiently rebuffed the plaintiff's allegations regarding the requested evidence.

In a similar Virginia case, parents sought help for their infant child's possible blood disorder.[20] After a series of routine shots, but apparently before any bleeding screen was ordered, the child developed bruises on various portions of his body. On two occasions, notwithstanding an intervening visit by the parents to another physician, the physician apparently berated the family extensively for having abused their child. It was later learned, according to complaints filed by the parents, that the child's problems resulted from hemophilia. The parents brought suit, alleging infliction of mental and physical stress, humiliation and embarrassment. The physician defended on the basis of the immunity provisions found in the state's abuse reporting act. The appellate court denied the physician's motion for dismissal on the basis that immunity clauses are narrowly construed, and that the doctor's communications to the parents were disproportionate to the occasion, providing a basis for allegations of malicious intent.

FAILURE TO PROPERLY SELECT
OR MONITOR PLACEMENT

Cases under this heading have been brought on state and federal statutory and common law grounds. On the federal level, *Doe v. New York City Department of Social Services*[21] was brought as an action alleging violation of civil rights under 42

U.S.C., 1983. The jury found that an agency charged with monitoring a foster home in which a child was repeatedly sexually abused was not negligent in its supervision. In its decision the Court of Appeals for the Second Circuit remanded the case with an order for the trial court to hold a new trial and to give jury instructions differentiating between ordinary negligence and gross negligence.

Some state courts have also permitted a common law cause of action for inadequate selection or monitoring of foster homes.[22] The duty of protective services agencies to monitor foster placements is emphasized by decisions upholding removal from a foster home[23] and even removal from a prospective adoptive home[24] despite the fact that removal was opposed by the children's physical custodians. In each of the cases, physical harm up to, and including, death occurred. In contrast, recovery for harm resulting from long-term "warehousing" of children in foster care facilities has been rejected by at least one court.[25]

WRONGFUL REMOVAL OR DETENTION OF CHILDREN

Sims v. State Department of Public Welfare[26] may be the best known case of this topic and is important even though no damages were sought. A federal district court ruled that significant portions of the Texas reporting statute were unconstitutional, including provisions allowing a ten-day temporary custody without a hearing, without notice to parents and without protections associated with use of the state's central registry for child abuse reports.

In a case involving a similar situation, *Griffin v. Pate*,[27] police followed up a school report of possible abuse to three children and sought to take the children in protective custody at home. The police were obstructed in their attempt to take one child into custody by the plaintiffs. Following prolonged discussion and some physical confrontation, additional police officers arrived and arrested the plaintiffs for interference with police officers in performance of their duties. The plaintiffs brought suit, alleging outrageous conduct, trespass and negligence. These claims were rejected by the court. The appellate court upheld the trial court's findings, and further ruled that since no evidence was presented to rebut the statutory presumption of the officer's good faith, the defendant's immunity clause, by implication, was valid.

The defense of the governmental or municipal immunity has been unsuccessfully raised in child protective cases by police,[28] and by veteran's hospital employees under the Federal Tort Claims Act (involving failure to warn a potential victim of a mental patient).[29] The widely reported case of *Stump v. Sparkman,* involving a judge's order for sterilization of a retarded minor, eventually resulted in the Supreme Court upholding the claim of judicial immunity.[30]

OTHER CIVIL ACTIONS

Since children usually cannot sign legally binding contracts, it seems unlikely that many suits will be brought against professionals or agencies for breach of contract by children directly. However, since children are third party beneficiaries to contracts signed by their guardians, cases based on contract law may become more prevalent as attention is directed to children's legal interests. Older children, of course, are more able to obtain recovery through contract theory, even against their own parents.[31]

At a time of economic downturn, suits seeking equitable remedies may prove less attractive to both litigants and their attorneys. There are, however, enough cases in which injunctions have been ordered against state agencies operating correctional institutions for youths,[32] or facilities for the mentally retarded, physically handicapped, or mentally ill,[33] to establish this as a viable alternative to the kinds of actions discussed earlier in this article.

CRIMINAL LIABILITY FOR PROFESSIONAL
MALPRACTICE

Colorado appears to be the first state in which social workers have been convicted for failing to carry out official duties;[34] however, there have been criminal indictments in several states. In Pueblo, Colorado, the case worker for a child, who was previously placed in foster care and subsequently returned home, had been in an accident and was working part-time. Calls from the school on two occasions to report suspicious bruises were not passed on to the worker. The worker never went to see the child, and the child choked to death on her own vomit.[35] The case was heard by a judge without a jury, and the judge convicted the social worker for the statutory offense of second degree official misconduct.[36] The conviction was later overturned on the basis that only "transactional" and not "use" immunity was then possible under Colorado statutory law and, therefore, the social worker could not be forced to testify against her supervisor, as had occurred, while her own appeal was pending.[37] The supervisor for the case worker was also indicted on official misconduct charges and was also convicted. This conviction was subsequently overturned on the basis that the official misconduct statute was void for vagueness.[38]

In Kentucky during June 1980, a child protective services supervisor, two case workers and a physician were charged with failing to report child abuse, and the supervisor and one worker were additionally charged with one count each of official misconduct. The case resulted when a three-year-old child died of burns six months after having suffered a fracture. This finding had not been reported to the department or the police by the hospital. All charges were eventually dismissed.[39] In September 1980, an El Paso grand jury indicted three employees of the Texas Department of Human Resources on eighteen counts each of criminal negligence in failing to perform legally mandated responsibilities.[40] These indictments were eventually quashed.[41] The case of *Florida v. Groff*[42] in which a psychiatrist was prosecuted (but later exonerated) for failing to report, has been noted above. A psychologist in Denver, Colorado, pleaded *nolo contendere* to misdemeanor charges of failing to report; and during 1982, a Colorado Springs school principal was convicted under the same child abuse reporting statute. At the trial, it was shown that the principal knew that one of his teachers, a retired military officer, was reported to have molested several of his ten-year-old students.[43]

All of the charges thus far were brought under criminal statutes. But *Pope v. State*[44] involved a common law offense, misprision of felony, based on child abuse. The Maryland Court of Appeals overturned the conviction, holding that the crime of misprision of felony no longer exists in Maryland.[45] The discussion by the majority, as well as by the dissent, indicated that any criminal convictions for child-abuse-related offenses are likely to be statutorily based.

ACCOUNTABILITY OF THE CHILD'S REPRESENTATIVE

A variety of means for holding the child's legal representative accountable is discussed in this section. The scarcity of cases directly on point is probably more a symptom of the difficulties that incompetents, including children, are likely to encounter in holding others responsible for their losses than an assurance that all children in all cases are being adequately represented. This author knows of few specifics about any case in which an attorney has been civilly liable for failure to carry out minimal duties toward a child/client. Before such actions can be brought successfully, statutes mandating duties for attorneys and others representing children will have to be enacted. Otherwise, the numerous potential barriers to suing will be extremely difficult to overcome due to the relative scarcity of precedent suits. For example, the standards of performance that should be applied are unknown, as is the yardstick to measure the degree of performance.

Ethics or grievance committees are the recognized mechanisms for dealing with misdeeds by lawyers. However, there are some special, natural obstacles to their being useful to ensure the accountability of the child's legal representative. It is unlikely that the child, by reason of his or her incompetency, will bring the attorney or guardian *ad litem* to task. Because there is seldom money for child representation, attorneys and courts are often reluctant to burden the attorney willing to take on such cases with demands for adequate performance. The theory seems to be that any pressure will leave the child with no legal representation at all. Furthermore, as anyone who has attempted to hold a fellow member of the bar accountable probably can attest, the disciplinary process is unpleasant and requires uncompensated time and energy. Formal grievance committee meetings leading to exoneration, warnings or disbarment seen remote to child representatives, at present.

Statutory guidelines for the guardians *ad litem* are a relatively inexpensive, but important, way to put the child's representative on notice as to what is required. The guidelines can also include clauses empowering the representative to take certain appropriate actions, avoiding needless litigation about questions such as rights of discovery, jury *voir dire,* introduction of evidence and witnesses and ancillary suits.[46]

The courts can perform a crucial role in this area. Given the special nature of the role of the guardian *ad litem,*[47] no entity is more routinely important than the courts to holding the guardian *ad litem* accountable. Some examples of the techniques used by judges are worth relating. The letter of appointment has been used by some courts to state the court's expectations, to assign responsibilities and to note legal powers of the guardian *ad litem.* With this method, the court can base the appointment and eventual compensation on clear, prestated terms, which both eases any disputes about the scope of the task of the guardian *ad litem* and puts the representative on routine notice.

In cases where incompetence, inattention or abuse of discretion is manifest, the court could send a letter to the grievance committee; although, for reasons already discussed, it would probably choose not to do so. A more workable remedy might be the appointment of a master to supervise the representative's work. This would be especially helpful where the guardian *ad litem* or attorney is willing, perhaps eager, but simply not fully qualified for a particular case. It permits a learning relationship and an assessment after the case as to whether this type of law should be practiced by the particular representative in the future. If it is determined that improvement is unlikely, circumstances involving the health or safety of the child may require that the representative be asked to resign, or that removal from the case be ordered with due process.

To avoid some of the educational aspects of oversight, encouragement of training programs for children's representatives is essential. There are now a number of training programs available, including those of the National Legal Resource Center for Child Advocacy and Protection of the American Bar Association[48] and the National Association of Counsel for Children.[49]

POLICY CONSIDERATIONS FOR JUDICIAL AND LEGAL ADMINISTRATORS

An important policy consideration for the legal system is the assurance of competent legal representation. The intricacies of assuring competent representation for children are such that it may be difficult for most courts of general jurisdiction to stay abreast of rapid developments and special knowledge demanded in the field of children's law. Often judgments in this area not only depend on expertise from a wide variety of disciplines, including medicine, psychology or psychiatry, social work and child development, but also demand special attention to matters usually associated with probate, mental health, family court or juvenile court procedures (especially with respect to the special issues of incompetency, substituted judgment and ethics). A homogenization of specialty courts to general jurisdictional status should be considered with great caution to avoid risks to children.

Unlike medicine, which holds postmortems routinely as a teaching device, postmortems on legal cases generally occur only on a basis quite removed from the actual event; for example, in continuing legal education. A few occur in very formal and adversarial court proceedings. However, the nonaccusatory and interdisciplinary examination of all aspects of a case of a child's death or injury, due to parental or institutional abuse or neglect, could decrease the chance of its recurrence. The analogy between the patient treated by a complex hospital system of surgeons, nurses, anesthesiologists, laboratory technicians and others, and the child subjected to a complex system of abusing, neglecting, or abandoning parents, physicians, social workers, lawyers, courts, institutional caretakers and others, is close enough to suggest the need for considering a postmortem mechanism for mistakes in this area. One possible mechanism, the Child Protection Team, has already been used widely and has been adapted to the issues of agency and professional accountability in some jurisdictions.[50]

Finally, every state needs to examine thoroughly the various roles played by the child's legal representative, the funding for representation and the accountability of the legal representative. Rights without someone to articulate and enforce them leave their intended beneficiaries destitute of protection.[51]

FOOTNOTES

1. 131 Cal. Rptr. 69, 551 P.2d 389 (1976).
2. *Lipari v. Sears, Roebuck & Co.*, 497 F.Supp 185, 194-95 (D. Neb. 1980).
3. V. DeFrancis and C. Lucht, *Child Abuse Legislation in the 1970s,* American Humane Association, Denver: 1974, quoted in Douglas J. Besharov, "What Physicians Should Know About Child Abuse Reporting Laws," in *Child Abuse and Neglect: A Medical Reference,* N. S. Ellerstein (ed.), John Wiley and Sons, New York: 1981.
4. E.g.: Ark. Stat. Ann. section 42-816 (1977); Colo. Rev. Stat. section 19-10-104(4)(b)(1978); Iowa Code Ann. section 235 A 20 (1985); Mich. Comp. Laws Ann. section 722.633 (Supp. 1986); N.Y. Soc. Serv. Law tit. 6 section 420 (1983). An example of statutory language is the Colorado provision:

> Any person who willfully violates the provisions of subsection (1) of this section:
>   (a)   Commits a class 2 petty offense and, upon conviction thereof, shall be punished by a fine not to exceed two hundred dollars;
>   (b)   Shall be liable to damages proximately caused thereby.
> Colo. Rev. Stat. section 19-10-104 (4)(1978).

5. *Landeros v. Flood, supra* note 1, at 392.
6. 131 Cal. Rptr. 14, 551 P.2d 334 (1976).
7. 168 N.J. Super. 466, 403 A.2d 500, 514-15 (1979).
8. 141 Cal. Rptr. 92, 95 (App. 1977).
9. 45 Md. App. 718, 415 A.2d 625, 630-31 (1980).
10. 409 So.2d 44 (Fla. App. 1981).
11. Id. at 45.
12. *Derrick v. Ontario Community Hospital,* 47 Cal App.3d 145, 120 Cal. Rptr. 566, 572 (1975); *Jones v. Stanko,* 118 Ohio St. 147, 160 N.E. 456, 458 (1928).
13. *Skillings v. Allen,* 173 N.W. 663, 664 (Minn. 1919); *Gully Hartford Accident and Indemnity Co.,* 337 So.2d 420, 421 (Fla. App. 1976). See, generally Donald C. Bross, "Legal Aspects of STD Control," *Sexually Transmitted Diseases,* Holmes, et al (eds.), McGraw-Hill, New York: 1978.
14. ATLA Reporter 24(2):76 (1981).
15. *Buege v. Iowa,* No. 20521 (July 30, 1980); *Fischer v. Iowa Department of Social Services,* No. V1664.280 (February 18, 1980).
16. Petition at Law, *Buege v. Iowa, supra.*
17. *City of Jacksonville v. Florida First Nat'l Bank,* 339 So.2d 632, 634 (Fla. 1976).

18. Id. at 636 (Boyd, J. dissenting).

19. *Martin v. County of Weld,* 598 P.2d 532, 535 (Colo. 1979).

20. *Austin v. French,* No. 80-114(d) (W.D. Va. March 23, 1981).

21. 649 F.2d 134 (2d Cir. 1981).

22. *Bartels v. Westchester,* 429 N.Y.S.2d 906, 909 (App. Div. 1980); *Koepf v. York,* 251 N.W.2d 866, 871 (Neb. 1977); *Vonner v. State,* 273 So.2d 252, 255-56 (La 1973); *Elton v. County of Orange,* 3 Cal App. 3d 1053, 84 Cal. Rptr. 27, 29 (1970).

23. *Gill v. Smith,* 382 N.Y.S.2d 626, 627-68 (N.Y. Sup. Ct. 1976).

24. *In re Adoption of Doe,* 444 P.2d 800, 804 (Wash. 1968).

25. *Child v. Beame,* 412 F.Supp. 593, 603-05 (S.D.N.Y. 1976). *Note:* But see *Bradford v. Davis* 626 P.2d 1376 (Or. 1981). Case settled for $90,000 when 17-year-old sued because "agency failed to take reasonable actions to find an adoptive home."

26. 438 F.Supp. 1179 (1977), rev'd on other grounds sub nom; *Moore v. Sims,* 442 U.S. 415 (1979).

27. *Griffin v. Pate,* 644 P.2d 51 (Colo. 1982).

28. *City of Jacksonville v. Florida First National Bank, supra* note 17, at 633.

29. *Lipari v. Sears, Roebuck & Co., supra* note 2 at 195.

30. 435 U.S. 349 (1978).

31. See *Lawyer's Alert* 1:6, 1982.

32. *Nelson v. Heyne,* 491 F.2d 352, 362 (7th Cir. 1974); *Morales v. Turman,* 383 F.Supp. 53, 126 (E.D. La. 1974).

33. *Gary W. v. Louisiana,* 437 F.Supp. 1209 (E.D. La. 1976).

34. See *Steinberger v. Dist. Ct.,* 596 P.2d 755 (Colo. 1979).

35. *Steinberger, supra* note 34; J.L. Spearly, "Caseworker Indictments—A Closer Look," *National Child Protection Services Newsletter* 3(4):6, 1981.

36. *Steinberger, supra* note 34; Colo. Rev. Stat. section 18-8-405 (1978) states:

1. [A] public servant commits second degree official misconduct if he knowingly, arbitrarily, and capriciously:
    (a) Refrains from performing a duty imposed upon him by law or clearly inherent in the nature of his office, or:
    (b) Violates any statute or lawfully adopted rule or regulation relating to his office.
2. Second degree official misconduct is a class 1 petty offense.

37. In the words of the court:

Transaction immunity may be simply described as that which precludes prosecution for any transaction or affair about which a witness testifies. Use immunity, by contrast, is a grant with limitations. Rather than barring a subsequent related prosecution, it acts only to suppress, in any such prosecution, the witness' testimony and evidence derived directly or indirectly from that testimony.

Steinberger v. Dist. Ct., supra note 34 at 757, quoting *Wheeler v. Dist. Ct.* 184 Colo. 193, 519 P.2d 327 (1974).

38. *People v. Beruman,* 638 P.2d 789, 794 (Colo. 1982).

39. M.F. Casper and E.T. Hutchinson, "CPS Indictments in Kentucky and Their Aftermath," *National Child Protection Services Newsletter* 4:6, 1981.

40. *El Paso Times,* September 12, 1980, at 1.

41. *Caseworker Indictments, supra* note 35.

42. *Florida v. Groff, supra* note 10.

43. *Denver Post,* March 10, 1982 at 1, 11.

44. 38 Md. App. 520, 382 A.2d 880, 892 (1978), modified, 396 A.2d 1054 (Md. App. 1979).

45. 396 A.2d at 1078-79.

46. Colo. Rev. Stat. section 19-10-113(3) (1978) provides that in every child abuse and neglect case filed under this section:

> The court . . . shall appoint a guardian *ad litem* at the first appearance of the case in court. The guardian *ad litem* shall be provided with all reports relevant to the case made to or by any agency or person pursuant to this article and section 19-3-101 (4) and with reports of any examination of the responsible person made pursuant to this section. The court or the social services worker assigned to the case shall advise the guardian *ad litem* of significant developments in the case, particularly any further abuse or neglect of the child involved. The guardian *ad litem* shall be charged in general with the representation of the child's interests. To that end he shall make such further investigations as he deems necessary to ascertain the facts, talk with or observe the child involved, interview witnesses and the foster parents of the child, and examine and cross-examine witnesses in both the adjudicatory and dispositional hearings and may introduce and examine his own witnesses, make recommendations to the court concerning the child's welfare, and participate further in the proceedings to the degree necessary to adequately represent the child.

47. See B. S. Fraser, "Independent Representation of the Abused or Neglected Child: The Guardian *ad Litem,*" *California Western Law Review* 13:16, 1976.

48. National Legal Resource Center for Child Advocacy and Protection,

American Bar Association, 1800 M Street, N.W., Washington, D.C. 20036, (202) 331-2250.

49. C. Henry Kempe National Center for the Prevention and Treatment of Child Abuse and Neglect; National Association of Counsel for Children, 1205 Oneida St., Denver, CO. 80220, (303) 321-3963.

50. Donald C. Bross, "Multidisciplinary Teams and Effective Management of Abuse and Neglect," *Protecting Children Through the Legal System,* American Bar Association, Washington, D.C.: 1980.

51. Donald C. Bross and M. M. Munson, "Alternative Models of Legal Representation for Children," *Oklahoma City University Law Review* 5:561, 1980.

ADDITIONAL CASE REFERENCES

The following cases serve to update and supplement the references footnoted in this chapter, which was previously published.

FAILURE TO REPORT: *O'Keefe v. Dr. Pablo Osario,* Cook Co. Cir. Ct. No. 70L-14884, July 24, 1984 (award of $186,851 against doctor who failed to report abuse regarding grandchild of his secretary); *Robison v. Wichal,* No. 37607 San Luis Obispo Co. Super. Ct., Cal. 1972 (case against four doctors and police chief who failed to report severely battered boy settled out of court for $1 million).

FAILURE TO INVESTIGATE REPORT PROPERLY: *Deshaney v. Winnebago Co.,* No. 85-C-310, E.d. Wisc., June 20, 1986 (civil rights suit against Dept. of Soc. Serv. for failure to protect child from abuse after several reports dismissed as court found no special relationship existed between defendants and child); however, see *Estate of Bailey v. County of York,* 768 F.2d 503, 3rd Cir. 1985 (court found special relationship existed where child who had been temporarily placed in protective custody was returned to mother's custody and died from beating); *Williams v. State,* 376 N.W.2d 117, Mich. App. 1985 (immunity granted to Soc. Serv. regarding alleged failure to intervene where child died of starvation after reports of neglect); *Sorichetti v. City of N.Y.,* 482 N.E.2d 70, 492 N.Y.S.2d 591, 1985 (App. Ct. reduced award against police from $3 million to $2 million in case regarding negligent failure to provide reasonable protection to six-year-old attacked by father); *Thurman v. City of Torrington,* 595 F.Supp. 1521, U.S.D.C. 1984 (police force that failed to respond to reports of wife abuse ordered to pay $2.6 million damages; case settled out of court for $1.9 million); *Jensen v. Conrad,* 747 F.2d 195, 4th Cir. 1984 (immunity granted).

FAILURE TO PROPERLY SELECT OR MONITOR PLACEMENT: *Taylor v. Ledbetter,* 791 F.2d 881, 11th Cir. 1986 (child overdosed in foster care; suit against Soc. Serv. for failure to properly investigate placement dismissed; no allegations of specific knowledge of deficiencies); *Doe v. N.Y.C. Dept. of Soc. Serv.,* 709 F.2d 782, 2nd Cir. 1983 (on remand jury awarded $225,000 approved by Ct. of Appeals).

WRONGFUL REMOVAL OR DETENTION OF CHILDREN: *Duchesne v. Sugarman,* 566 F.2d 817, 2d Cir. 1977 (liability for failure to obtain judicial ratification of removal for three years).

OTHER CIVIL ACTIONS: *Doe v. Hennepin Co.,* 623 F.Supp. 982, D. Minn. 1985 (court-appointed psychologist immune in civil rights action brought by disgruntled parents); *Cavello v. Sherburne-Earlville School Dist.,* 494 N.Y.S.2d 466, N.Y.S.C. 1985 (school district could be liable for failure to supervise children resulting in plaintiff's child's emotional distress); *Wolfe v. New Mexico Dept. of Human Serv.,* 575 F.Supp. 346, D.N.M. 1983 (dependent and neglected children may maintain class action for failure to develop permanent placement plans).

ACCOUNTABILITY OF THE CHILD'S REPRESENTATIVE: *Dryden v. Coulon,* 378 N.W.2d 767, Mich. App. 1985 (friend of court not civilly liable for failure to properly investigate child's environment; grievance procedure established); *In re Scott Co.,* 618 F.Supp. 1534, D. Minn. 1985 (guardian ad litem granted immunity as integral part of judicial process).

PART III

Standard Procedures
for the Child Advocate

SUGGESTED GUIDELINES FOR THE GUARDIAN *AD LITEM*

National Association of Counsel for Children*

STATUTORY BASIS (COLORADO EXAMPLE)

The court in every case filed under this section shall appoint a guardian *ad litem* at the first appearance of the case in court. The guardian *ad litem* shall be provided with all reports relevant to the case made to or by any agency or person pursuant to this article and section 19-3-101(4) and with reports of any examination of the responsible person made pursuant to this section. The court or the social services worker assigned to the case shall advise the guardian *ad litem* of significant developments in the case, particularly any further abuse or neglect of the child involved. The guardian *ad litem* shall be charged in general with the representation of the child's interests. To that end he shall make such further investigations as he deems necessary to ascertain the facts, talk with or observe the child involved, interview witnesses and the foster parents of the child, and examine and cross-examine

*Originally drafted by the Standards and Training Committee of the National Association of Counsel for Children: Elaine Edinburg, Celia Katz, Paul Linton and Russ Richardson.

199

witnesses in both the adjudicatory and dispositional hearings and may introduce and examine his own witnesses, make recommendations to the court concerning the child's welfare, and participate further in the proceedings to the degree necessary to adequately represent the child. (Colo. Rev. Stat. 19-10-113(3))

1. At the time you first receive a phone call from the court and decide you will accept an appointment, take down the name of the case, the civil action number, the next hearing date and the purpose of that hearing, the attorneys of record and the Child Protective Services caseworker, if known to the court.

2. Do not wait for the papers to arrive from the court file more than one week. (If a hearing is scheduled within a couple of days, obviously, you cannot wait the one week.) Check the court file for papers and obtain copies of anything in the court file, including all minutes. Often the clerk does not send everything.

INDEPENDENT INVESTIGATION

1. Contact the caseworker if known. If the caseworker's name is not known, check with Child Protective Services by providing the case name and number. Often there are two separate workers on the case. Sometimes an intake worker is initially assigned during the first 48 hours, followed by assignment of an ongoing caseworker. Make sure that you have talked to both workers and that you are fully informed of the events which took place while either or both of them was on the case. Any time caseworkers are not available, contact the supervisor.

    ■ Review the caseworker's file and all relevant information.
    ■ Obtain the names and addresses of the foster homes where the child or children is (are) placed. If this

information is not available through the caseworker, go to the foster home unit of Child Protective Services.

- If any injuries have occurred, obtain the names of hospitals, attending physicians, the chief of services or other active people, e.g., social worker, child protection team. Also, obtain any color photographs available.
- Obtain visitation schedules. If there are none, inquire as to why not.

2. Contact the attorney for the respondent parents. Obtain all background and history reasonably relevant. The parents' stories may be quite different from that of Child Protective Services.

- Request permission from the attorney to arrange for a home visit at the child's home. It probably would be helpful if you could arrange to drop in at an unannounced time.
- If feasible and appropriate, and the child is with the parents, you may ask to have the child brought to court.
- Obtain the names of family doctors, counselors and people involved in ongoing treatment plans.

3. Contact the child.

- If under two years of age, visit the child and make observations wherever he or she is, i.e., foster home, relative's home or parents' home.
- Children over four years of age, or old enough to communicate, should be interviewed alone. Try to ascertain what the child's feelings actually are. Often the child will echo the opinions of the foster parents or the caseworker while harboring his own independent thoughts!
- If a child is in foster placement and visitations are ongoing, the guardian *ad litem* should arrange a visit to observe the interaction between the parents and the child.

4. You may make other contacts through school personnel, visiting nurse services, homemakers, parent aides, drug or alcohol counselors, neighbors, ministers or babysitters, etc.

5. When a dependency and neglect petition is filed, the coordinator of a county Child Protection Team *must* notify the guardian *ad litem in writing* as to:

    - The reason for initiating the petition,
    - Suggestions as to the optimum disposition of this particular case, and
    - Suggested therapeutic treatment and social services available within the community for the subject child and the responsible person.

Investigation will be as complete and revealing as your efforts permit. This is an essential part of your work.

PREPARATION FOR HEARINGS

At any stage you enter the proceeding, make sure that you have discovered what resulted from any previous hearing.

1. *Temporary custody hearing.* Determine whether the outcome of the hearing was appropriate. If not, you may file your own motion for change of custody. This motion must be based on a change of circumstances or new evidence. This may be done by setting a forthwith hearing and assuring that notice is given to all parties. The immediate protection and care of the child is the paramount concern. This may also apply to inappropriate foster care.

2. *Return on Summons and/or pretrial hearing.* At the return on summons, parents ordinarily are advised of their rights, and the court affirms its jurisdiction over the parties. The return on summons may be combined with the pretrial when there has already been a temporary custody hearing.

At this time the petitioner will submit a written list of witnesses and documents. The guardian *ad litem* should submit separate statements whenever necessary. Note that this step is the only way to be able to assure that the witnesses you may wish to have will be there.

The pretrial will also define and limit what issues are to be tried in the case. At this time, it is appropriate to check on whether subpoenas will be issued by the Protective Services Agency for certain witnesses, and which witnesses will need to be subpoenaed directly by the guardian *ad litem*.

- *Informal adjustment.* There may be a statutory limit on an informal adjustment, as opposed to a continued petition where there is no adjudication. The assumption implicit in some statutes is that informal adjustment will occur before the petition is filed; but this is rarely observed in practice. The court may, however, continue to review and supervise the case for an indefinite period of time. Both the informal adjustment and the continued petition must be based on admissions made by the parents. The guardian *ad litem* should take a role, and perhaps *must* take a role; but the statute may specify that the Department of Social Services shall agree to this category of resolution.
- *Right to a jury trial.* Some statutes provide the guardian *ad litem* to request a jury trial.
- *Negotiation.* The parents may admit one allegation of the petition, and all the others will be stricken, including striking the prayer for termination of parental rights. Sometimes this may not be in the child's best interest. You should always be aware of what the plea negotiations are.
- *Alternatives.* The following alternatives should be considered at the time of the pretrial:

  — Motion for psychological evaluation,
  — Motion for home study,
  — Motion for increase or decrease of visitation,

— Motion for child's psychological evaluation,
— Motion for child's developmental testing, or
— Motion for child's neurological study.

If any of these alternatives seem necessary, they may be requested at this time. The guardian *ad litem* should also be involved in any continuing discovery that is supplied by either the petitioner or the respondent. This would include being notified and advised of any staffing to be held concerning the status of the minor child. If the evidence is vague or contradictory, it is essential that the guardian *ad litem* pursue pretrial discovery.

■ You should always check on the status of the respondent father, especially if the case appears to be heading towards termination of parental rights. If he is unavailable or not a party to the action through service, you should check on publication.

3. *Adjudicatory hearing.* The guardian *ad litem* must be prepared to present an appropriate case, whether limited or extensive in nature.

■ You have a right to cross-examine the witnesses.
■ You have a right to make opening and closing statements.
■ You have a right to call witnesses of your own and introduce independent evidence. It is questionable whether or not you have a right to *voir dire* the jury.
■ You may make a request for a continuance, if the necessary witnesses have not been properly subpoenaed or are unavailable at that time.

If the adjudicatory hearing results in no finding of dependency, the case is dismissed at that point.

At the close of the adjudicatory hearing, the guardian *ad litem* may make a motion for visitation to be either enlarged or decreased, and/or a motion for psychological

testing if it is indicated at this time. You may request an
independent evaluation at any time it seems appropriate.

4. *Dispositional stage.*   At the dispositional hearing the court
    will determine what will happen to the child and will enter
    any appropriate orders to establish a treatment plan to
    remedy the problems that initially brought the case before
    the court. Options available to the court include the
    following:

    ■ Continuation of foster care;
    ■ Return of the child with supervision of Child Protec-
       tive Services to the legal or physical custody of the
       parents;
    ■ Therapy or counseling of the parent either alone or
       with the child;
    ■ Treatment of the child, for example, through speech
       therapy, therapeutic play school, medical regimes,
       psychotherapy or group therapy;
    ■ Placement with relatives; institutional care or residen-
       tial treatment as deemed appropriate for the child's
       needs; or
    ■ Termination of the parent–child legal relationship (see
       Case Law for criteria).

    The dispositional report prepared by the caseworker
prior to the dispositional hearing should be available ten
days prior to the hearing date. If the dispositional hearing
is approaching and you have not heard from the caseworker, you should call and find out when the report will
be available to you. You may request a continuance if the
report remains unavailable and you do not have time to
properly prepare. You can submit your own written report
at the dispositional stage.

HELPFUL HINTS

Request an independent evaluation of the parents and the
child whenever it seems that the Child Protective Service or

respondent's evaluation is biased or inappropriate. Important questions include the cognitive and emotional status of
the child; to what extent the child's status, relative to his
age group, is good or bad due to the acts or neglect of his
parent(s); the response or likely response of the parent(s)
to therapy; and, most specifically, the capacity or incapacity of the respondent(s) to adequately parent the child(ren)
in question.

2. There should probably be a conference on the terms and
    conditions of the informal adjustment between the case-
    worker, the client, the respondent's attorney, the guardian
    ad litem and, if possible, the city attorney. Make sure that
    this is a feasible plan and take a role in drafting the
    agreement. Make sure that the language and the terms of
    the agreement are consistent.

3. Try to ensure that whenever a staffing is held that you, as
    guardian *ad litem,* are notified of the time and place.

4. Any time there is an informal adjustment the guardian *ad
    litem* can continue to check on the case status and, if an
    injurious situation has arisen, the case can be reopened by
    the guardian *ad litem.*

5. Background reading may prove very valuable, or even
    essential, in a given case. Some useful texts include: Helfer
    and Kempe (eds.), *Child Abuse and Neglect: The Family and
    The Community* (1976); Helfer and Kempe (eds.), *Helping
    the Battered Child and His Family* (1975); Besharov, *Juvenile
    Justice Advocacy: Practice in a Unique Court;* Freud, Gold-
    stein, Solnit (eds.), *Beyond the Best Interests of the Child*
    (1973); R. S. Kempe and C. H. Kempe, *Child Abuse*
    (1978).

6. Do not hesitate to consult with the membership of the
    National Association of Counsel for Children in Denver,
    Colorado. The office can provide names of any local
    members known to the national office.

Guidelines for Custody and Dispositional Hearings in Abuse and Neglect Cases

Jon L. Lawritson, Esq.

CUSTODY HEARING

The following lists the minimal elements of concern to the court in making custody orders. Custody, of course, may be decided at many points during the dependency and neglect process and may be a specific aspect of the dispositional hearing. This is not an exhaustive listing, but it will provide some direction to guardians preparing for such hearings. Remember that the court needs all relevant information and that live witnesses with directly observed information are generally given more weight than are written reports or summaries.

A. Injury
   ■ Results of physical exam,
   ■ Results of x-rays,
   ■ Results of lab tests,
   ■ Color photographs, and
   ■ Injury history given by:
      — mother,
      — father,
      — child,
      — witness, and/or
      — police.

B.   History of each parent or adult household member
      ■ Was parent abused or deprived as a child? When?
        How?
      ■ Record of mental illness. When? Diagnosis? Prior
        hospitalization?
      ■ Difficulties with the law? When? Type (assaults, drug
        abuse, alcohol related)?
      ■ Prior reports of abuse or neglect?
      ■ Violent temper outbursts towards child or other
        family members?
      ■ None of the above.

C.   How do parents view the child or children?
      ■ Inappropriate or rigid expectations?
      ■ Harsh or unusual punishment?
      ■ Child seems difficult or provocative?
      ■ Child unwanted?
      ■ None of the above—very appropriate view of
        children.

D.   How does child view parents?
      ■ Is the child attached to the parent(s)? Foster par-
        ent(s)? Therapist(s)? Others (name and describe
        relationship).
      ■ Is the child old enough to have a stated view of his
        parent(s) and, if so, what is it?
      ■ Is the attachment of the child to the parent viewed by
        professionals as healthy or unhealthy?

E.   Special problems or characteristics of the child
      ■ At what stage of development is the child and how
        does the subject child stand with relationship to other
        children of his or her age?
      ■ What changes have been observed in the child before,
        during and after stays with the foster family and the
        biologic family?
      ■ Does the child exhibit any sign(s) of mental or
        emotional disorders or disabilities?

- Is the child particularly attached or markedly unatt-ached to siblings or other children in a way that may affect the best placement for the child?
- Under what circumstances, especially as to placement, will the child best be able to receive any necessary treatment services?

F. Are there any present crises or stresses in family?

G. Socially isolated family or socially active?

H. Why safety of child can't be assured at home:
- Crisis situation needs to be calmed;
- Severe mental illness in home;
- Parents will not allow anyone in home;
- No one to care for child;
- Violent person in home needs treatment commenced;
- Parent(s) needs to obtain parenting skills, for example, failure-to-thrive, inability to deal with emotional problems of child;
- Child needs special care not available in home;
- Age of child; and/or
- Other.

I. Alternative methods of insuring safety of child available.

J. Length of child's probable stay away from home.

K. Other children in home and their probable safety.

L. The guardian should be aware that any changes in the child may be the best evidence of what is wrong with the type of parenting the child has received. Once treatment or a placement has taken place over time, a further assessment may be needed to describe the changes in the child and, if possible, to attribute the observed changes to the good or bad effects of the child's being in the biological parents' home or the foster home setting. The guardian must be aware of the need to be very precise in outlining the questions that are to be asked and answered by an evaluating psychologist, psychiatrist or social worker.

M.   Is an independent evaluation of the respondent parent or child indicated?

DISPOSITIONAL HEARING

The fact sheets of the dispositional report normally should contain the following items:

- Dependency Action (court);
- Number;
- Date of Hearing;
- Names, addresses and birthdates of children;
- Names and addresses of parents;
- Names and addresses of other respondents;
- Names and birthdates of other household members; and
- Names and addresses of other relatives who may be concerned in planning for children, for example, grandparents, uncles and aunts, etc.;
- Persons expected at the hearing; and
- Persons present at the staffing and their professional function, for example, pediatrician, guardian *ad litem*, counsel for respondent(s), etc.

The body of the report should summarize the following:

A.   *Why the case is in court.*   Brief description of the facts, proven or admitted (physical abuse, failure-to-thrive, sexual abuse, medical care neglect, intentional drugging or poisoning, emotional abuse, abandonment, lack of supervision, physical neglect, etc.).

B. *History of child.* Brief history of custody, placements, physical problems, emotional problems, special needs, school placement or daycare.

C. *History of mother.* Brief discussion of social history, physical problems, emotional problems, marital problems, childrearing practices, view of child and view of court involvement.

D. *History of father.* Contents should be the same as history of mother.

E. *History of other household members.* Contents should be the same as history of mother and father.

F. *Family Crises.* Current personal or emotional crises in the family might include a death, desertion or divorce; recent moves; inadequate housing—heat, water—and lack of money, food or job, etc.

G. *Outside Contacts.* These include social and agency contacts with *each* family member or other person(s) in household. Attach reports, if any are available.

A guardian should be aware that special attention must be given to potential caretakers. If foster care is proposed, the guardian must be assured that the foster care placement is indeed appropriate and safe. If relatives are to be used, the guardian should be satisfied that these relatives do not themselves represent a continuation of the child's problem. Thus, grandparents may be entirely appropriate caretakers for an abused and neglected child or, in contrast, may represent merely an earlier, battering generation.

H. *Treatment plan.* Often the concern about a treatment plan focuses on the parents. The assumption, explicit or unstated, is that once the parent is treated, all the child's needs will be met. Once a child has been the subject of abuse and/or neglect, however, the guardian must consider not only the needs of the parents for treatment, but any special needs that have arisen for the child.

The treatment plan for the parents should contain the following elements.

- Identification of the causes or conditions that resulted in the court acquiring jurisdiction as to each family member.
- The course of treatment or counseling appropriate for each member of the household, including the children who are the subject of the action. The course of treatment should include a statement as to for whom, when, and where the treatment is to take place.
- If the child is in protective custody:

  — Reasons why the child should remain in custody or why the child should return home.
  — If the child is to remain in custody, one should consider the probable duration of the custody, whether visitation should be allowed and under what conditions, and the goals to be reached by the parent(s) and/or child(ren) prior to the return home.
  — The guardian should consider the adequacy of the foster home. Because there may be a lack of good foster homes, and because the Department of Social Services is also responsible for the adequacy of foster care homes, a child may not necessarily be placed in the best foster home care available at a particular moment. The guardian should question himself and others about the safety of the home, and whether the special needs of the child represented are being met in that foster care home. For example, a certain child may need a father figure, and thus, a single foster mother home would be inappropriate for such a child. If a child has a special need for stimulation, there should be an assurance that such stimulation

is provided, within the reasonable resources of a Department of Social Services.

— There should be a plan for monitoring and evaluating progress toward a conclusion of the proceedings, with a recommended date of termination of the court's jurisdiction, a suggested time for the next review, who will report problems to the court, the length of probable treatment or counseling and the goals to be reached. The guardian may wish to consider whether or not *a time certain* can, or must, be recommended for a final determination and permanent placement by the court. By not making a strong statement on the need for a definite time determination, especially as to very young children, the guardian is increasing the chances that the child's permanent placement will be indefinitely delayed.

— The guardian should consider whether parental rights of either or both parents should be preserved or terminated, and consider the reasons for that decision.

— Financial ability of parents to pay for, or contribute to, the cost of treatment and/or care of their child(ren) should be evaluated.

— The guardian should determine whether alternative treatment plans for each person involved exist, what these plans might be, and the advantages and costs of each plan.

Selected Legal Forms

The following forms are included for reference only and may be adapted for use in dependency, abuse and neglect cases on a case by case basis.

Not all of these forms will be used in any given case, and under some circumstances, others may be required. However, these selected legal documents offer the guardian *ad litem* a general idea of the formats of those documents which are most likely to be needed.

GUARDIAN AD LITEM CHECKLIST

1. Case Name_____

2. Case Number_____ Court_____

                          County_____

3. Child's Name Date of Birth Address/Phone Foster Parents' Name

_____ _____ _____ _____
                        _____
_____ _____ _____ _____
                        _____
_____ _____ _____ _____
                        _____
_____ _____ _____ _____
                        _____

4. Mother's Name Date of Birth Address   Phone

_____ _____ _____ (Home)
                                       (Work)

5. Father's Name Date of Birth Address   Phone

_____ _____ _____ (Home)
                                       (Work)

6. Step-parents' Names Date of Birth Addresses/Phone

_____ _____ _____
                            _____
_____ _____ _____
                            _____

7. Pediatrician's Name   Address/Phone

_____   _____
                        _____

8. Teachers' Names   Address/Phone

_____   _____
                        _____
_____   _____
                        _____
_____   _____
                        _____

9. Social Worker's Name   Address/Phone

    Intake: _____   _____

    Outgoing: _____   _____
                                                    _____

10. Psychiatrist's Name   Address/Phone

    _____   _____
                                                    _____

11. Other Close Relatives Names   Addresses/Phone   Relationship

    _____   _____   _____

    _____   _____   _____

    _____   _____   _____

    _____   _____   _____
                                       _____

12. Names and Addresses of Friends of Child(ren)

    _____   _____

    _____   _____
                                                    _____

    _____   _____
                                                    _____

13. Allegations of Petitioner:_____

    _____

    _____

14. The following reports and documents are needed:

    _____

    _____

    _____

    _____

    _____

15. Potential Witnesses & Other Significant Persons:
    Name   Address/Phone   Significance

    _____   _____   _____
    _____   _____   _____
                       _____
    _____   _____   _____
                       _____
    _____   _____   _____
                       _____
    _____   _____   _____
                       _____
    _____   _____

16. Petitioner's Recommendation Concerning Placement, Treatment,
    Visitation, etc.

    _____
    _____
    _____

17. Guardian Ad Litem's recommendation concerning Placement,
    Treatment, Visitation, etc.

    _____
    _____
    _____
    _____

18. Guardian Ad Litem's Pleadings Filed With Court:

    Pleading   Date Filed   Hearing Date   Granted/Denied

    _____

    Motion for Costs_____

    Motion for Social
    Study_____

    Motion for
    Psychiatric Exam_____

    Motion for Temp.
    Custody Order/Change of Custody_____

18. Guardian <u>Ad</u> <u>Litem's</u> Pleadings Filed With Court: (cont'd)

Motion for Child
Support_____

Motion for
Psychological Exam_____

Motion for
Physical Exam_____

Other_____

19. Evidentiary Problems:_____

_____

_____

20. Trial Notebook Preparation:

Witnesses prepared for trial:

Name: What he/she will testify:

_____   _____

_____   _____

_____   _____

_____   _____

Checklist of the following:

Questions for voir dire prepared   ____

Opening Statement prepared   ____

Documents ready to introduce   ____

Witnesses prepared for trial   ____

Direct Examination prepared   ____

Cross Examination prepared   ____

Closing Statement prepared   ____

21. City or County Attorney (Name and Address/Phone):_____

_____

_____

22. Attorney(s) for (Name and Address/Phone):

Father_____

Mother_____

Other_____

23. Adjudication:_____

_____

_____

24. Terms of Treatment Plan:_____

_____

_____

25. Compliance:_____

_____

_____

26. Termination - Grounds:_____

_____

_____

27. Hearing Dates:
    Type of Hearing   Date

_____

_____

_____

_____

_____

_____

_____

_____

_____

GUARDIAN AD LITEM'S SUMMARY IN DIVORCE CASES

A. Developmental needs of child:

   1. Adjustment to home, school and community:_____

   _____

   _____

   2. Relationship between parents, siblings, others:_____

   _____

   _____

   3. Child's preference, reasons:_____

   _____

   _____

   4. Effect of change in custody (consider emotional impact,
       adaptability of child, long-term gain):_____

   _____

   _____

B. Parent's ability to meet child's needs:

   1. Quality and permanence of proposed environment for child:

   _____

   _____

   _____

   2. History of care for child/emotional ties:_____

   _____

   _____

   _____

   3. Capacity & Disposition for:

   Love and Affection:_____

   Care and Supervision:_____

   Support:_____

3. Capacity & Disposition for: (cont'd)

Education:_____

Other Special Needs:_____

_____

4. Physical Health:_____

_____

5. Mental Health:_____

_____

6. Social Adjustment:_____

_____

7. Educational Background:_____

_____

8. Employment/Salary:_____

_____

    Hours of Work:_____

9. Reasons for Wanting Custody:_____

_____

_____

10. Attitude Toward Visitation by Non-custodial Parent:_____

_____

_____

(Repeat form for each parent)

ORDER APPOINTING GUARDIAN AD LITEM

THIS MATTER having come on before the Court for the appointment of a Guardian ad Litem and the Court being fully advised and
finding that the best interest of the children demands the appointment of a Guardian ad Litem;

ORDERS

That _____, an attorney licensed to practice law
in the State of _____, be and hereby is appointed as
Guardian ad Litem for _____
_____.

DONE THIS ____ day of _____, 19___, in open Court NUNC
PRO TUNC for _____, 19___.

Recommended by: By the Court

_____   _____
                                   Judge

IN THE JUVENILE COURT IN AND FOR THE

CITY AND COUNTY OF _____

AND STATE OF _____

No.

In The Matter of The People In The Interest of _____ Child Upon The Petition of _____ Petitioner And Concerning _____ Respondents	)))))) INFORMAL ADJUSTMENT)))))))

    1. The respondents have been advised of and understand the
following statutory and constitutional rights:

        a. The nature of the statutory basis for dependency or
           neglect, to wit

           (1) That (his)(her)(their) parent, guardian or legal
               custodian has abandoned (him)(her)(them) or sub-
               jected (him)(her)(them) to mistreatment or abuse,
               or has suffered or allowed another to mistreat or
               abuse the child___ without taking lawful means
               to stop such mistreatment or abuse and prevent it
               from recurring;
           (2) That (he)(she)(they) lack(s) proper parental care
               through the actions or omissions of the parent,
               guardian or legal custodian;
           (3) That (his)(her)(their) environment is injurious
               to (his)(her)(their) welfare;
           (4) That (his)(her)(their) parent, guardian or legal
               custodian fails or refuses to provide proper care
               or necessary subsistence, education, medical care
               or other care necessary for (his)(her)(their)
               health, guidance or well being;
           (5) That said child___ (is)(are) homeless, without
               proper care or not domiciled with (his)(her)
               (their) parent, guardian or legal custodian
               through no fault of said parent, guardian or
               legal custodian.

b. The right to be represented by counsel at every stage of the proceedings.

c. The right to have a trial by jury.

2. It is voluntarily admitted, not as a result of any undue influence or coercion, that the following facts establish the jurisdiction of the Court:

3. That the admission contained in paragraph "2" hereinabove shall not be used in evidence if a petition is filed.

4. The parties desire to enter into an informal adjustment for a period of six (6) months from the date set forth hereinbelow to avoid, if possible, the filing of a petition.

5. Terms of the informal adjustment are set forth hereinafter on page 2.

6. It is understood that if the terms of this informal adjustment are carried out and said informal adjustment serves the best interests of the children there will be no further involvement of or with the Court.

7. Nothing in this agreement shall preclude any person at any time from requesting the Court to take formal action to protect the best interests of the children.

Terms of the Informal Adjustment

Signed and executed on _____(Date)

By_____
   Petitioner   Respondent

APPROVED:

_____   _____
Referee/Judge   Respondent

APPROVED AS TO FORM:

_____   _____
Attorney   Attorney

IN THE JUVENILE COURT

IN AND FOR THE CITY AND COUNTY OF _____

AND STATE OF _____

No._____

The People of the State of _____)
In the Interest of   )
)
)
_____)
                  Child_____   )
)
Upon the Petition of   )   MOTION FOR ISSUANCE OF A BENCH
)   WARRANT AND WRIT OF ASSISTANCE
)
_____)
                  Petitioner)
)
And Concerning   )
)
)
_____)
                  Respondent)

    Comes now the Petitioner and moves the Court, pursuant to (state statute), to issue a bench warrant for the apprehension of the child___

and as grounds therefore shows the Court that the welfare of said child___ requires that (he) (she) (they) be brought immediately into the custody of the Court as is evidenced by the attached exhibit__.

    Petitioner further moves for the issuance of a Writ of Assistance in aid of the bench warrant.

                          _____
                          Attorney for the Petitioner

IN THE JUVENILE COURT

IN AND FOR THE CITY AND COUNTY OF _____

AND STATE OF _____

No._____

```
The People of the State of _____)
In the Interest of               )
                                 )
                                 )
                                 )
_____)
                   Child_____    )
                                 )
Upon the Petition of             )        BENCH WARRANT AND
                                 )        WRIT OF ASSISTANCE
                                 )
                                 )
_____)
                   Petitioner )
                                 )
And Concerning                   )
                                 )
                                 )
                                 )
_____)
                   Respondent_)
```

THIS MATTER COMING ON TO BE HEARD this ____ day of _____, 19___, and the Court having read the motion for issuance of a bench warrant, examined the exhibit_ attached thereto, heard the statements of counsel, and being fully advised in the premises,

FINDS:

1. There is reasonable cause to believe that the welfare of child___ requires that (he) (she) (they) be brought immediately into the custody of the Court, pursuant to (state statute).

2. A writ of assistance, in aid of securing custody, should issue.

IT IS THEREFORE ORDERED, ADJUDGED AND DECREED:

1. Any law enforcement officer of the State of _____ is hereby authorized and ordered to apprehend and take into custody

wherever found, and thereafter deliver said child___ to a shelter facility designated by the Court or to any authorized representative of the Department of Social Services of the City and County of _____.

2. Any law enforcement officer in taking said child___ into custody may use and employ such force as may reasonably be necessary, including, but not limited to causing any building or enclosure in which the child___ (is) (are) reasonably believed to be located to be broken open in such manner as the law enforcement officer believes would cause the least damage to the building or enclosure.

3. The respondent_ herein may, upon 48 hours notice, request a hearing be held to determine whether the child___ should be further detained.

Done and signed in open Court this ____ day of _____,
19__

BY THE COURT:

_____
JUDGE

IN THE DISTRICT COURT WITHIN AND FOR

THE COUNTY OF _____ AND STATE OF _____

Juvenile No. J-_____ ; Div. _____

```
THE PEOPLE OF THE STATE OF _____ )
IN THE INTEREST OF:              )
                                 )
_____ )
                        Child___ )
                                 )
                                 )
ALLEGED TO BE (A) DEPENDENT      )          P E T I T I O N
OR NEGLECTED CHILD(REN):         )      IN DEPENDENCY AND NEGLECT
                                 )
_____ )
                                 )
                   Petitioner    )
                                 )
AND CONCERNING:                  )
                                 )
                                 )
_____ )
                                 )
                  Respondents    )
```

COMES NOW the Petitioner above-named, Caseworker for the _____
_____ Department of Social Services, and by and through ___
_____ , Attorneys for said Petitioner and said
Department of Social Services, and respectfully represents:

1. That the following named child(ren) reside(s) in or (is)
(are) present in the County of _____ and State of _____ :

Name   Sex   Date of Birth   Age

2. That the names and addresses of the Respondent(s) above-
named (is) (are) as follows:

Father:

Mother:

Stepfather/Stepmother:

Legal Guardian/Custodian:

3. That the above-named child(ren) (is) (are) dependent and neglected as defined in (state statute); specifically:

(a) Said child(ren)'s parent, guardian or legal custodian has abandoned said child(ren) or has subjected said child(ren) to mistreatment or abuse, or such parent, guardian or legal custodian has suffered or allowed another to mistreat or abuse the child(ren) without taking lawful means to stop such mistreatment or abuse and prevent it from recurring; OR

(b) Said child(ren) lack(s) proper parental care through the actions or omissions of the parent, guardian or legal custodian; OR

(c) Said child(ren)'s environment is injurious to such child(ren)'s welfare; OR

(d) Said child(ren)'s parent, guardian or legal custodian fails or refuses to provide proper or necessary subsistence, medical care, or any other care necessary for such child(ren)'s health, guidance or well-being; OR

(e) Said child(ren) (is) (are) homeless, without proper care, or not domiciled with his/her/their parent, guardian or legal custodian through no fault of such child(ren)'s parent, guardian or legal custodian; OR

THAT said child(ren) (is) (are) a neglected or abused child(ren) as defined in the (Child Protection Act), as defined in (state statute).

4. That the Petitioner herein is informed of the following facts which bring said child(ren) within the jurisdiction of this Court, to-wit:

WHEREFORE, Petitioner prays that a Summons be issued upon the parents of said child(ren)/the Respondents herein named, setting a time, date and place for hearing of this Petition; and that the within Petition be heard and a disposition be made by the Court, such disposition to include possible termination of parental rights, the filing of financial affidavits, and payment of support for the care and maintenance of the minor child(ren) in this matter; and for and along with such other Orders, remedies and relief as may be appropriate.

By:_____
Attorneys for Petitioner and the
County Department of Social
Services
Address:_____
Phone:_____

STATE OF _____)
COUNTY OF _____) ss:

    YOUR PETITIONER HEREIN, namely
of lawful age, being first duly sworn upon oath, deposes and
states: That I am the Petitioner above-named and whose name is
subscribed to this Petition; that I have read the above and foregoing PETITION IN DEPENDENCY AND NEGLECT; that I know the contents
thereof, and that same are true to the best of my personal
knowledge, information and belief.

PETITIONER _____

    Subscribed, sworn to and acknowledged before me this _____ day
of _____, A.D., 19___, by the above-named Petitioner.

    My Commission Expires:_____.

NOTARY PUBLIC _____

IN THE INTEREST OF   No._____   )   IN THE DISTRICT COURT OF

)

_____   )   _____ COUNTY

)

A CHILD   )   _____ JUDICIAL DISTRICT

ANSWER OF GUARDIAN AD LITEM

TO THE HONORABLE JUDGE OF SAID COURT:

    COMES NOW, _____, duly appointed Guardian ad Litem for the minor child, _____, and would respectfully show unto the Court as follows:

I

    On behalf of the minor child, the Guardian ad Litem herein would respectfully request that the Court review and consider with extreme gravity the testimony, evidence and facts of this case and proceed to a rendition of a Judgment with only the best interest of the minor child in mind.

II

    WHEREAS, a Guardian ad Litem has been appointed for the minor child, it is respectfully requested that reasonable attorney's fees be assessed.

    WHEREFORE, PREMISES CONSIDERED, your Movant herein, the Guardian ad Litem for the minor child, would respectfully move this Honorable Court for Judgment in keeping with the evidence produced at the time of trial, demonstrating the best interest of the minor child and further keeping in mind that the decision arrived at will affect the minor child in his development for many years to come. Movant further moves this Court to grant reasonable attorney's fees for his services.

                              Respectfully submitted,

                             _____

*Thanks to Reginald Hirsch for this and the following two forms.

No._____

IN THE INTEREST OF   )   IN THE DISTRICT COURT OF
)
_____   )   _____ COUNTY
)
A CHILD   )   _____ JUDICIAL DISTRICT

ORDER FOR INVESTIGATION

     BE IT REMEMBERED, on this the _____ day of _____,
19___, the above entitled and numbered cause having come on for
hearing, and came the parties in person and by their attorneys of
record, and the Court, being informed that this is a case involving
the custody of minor children, and the Court being desirous of
having a thorough investigation made as to the environment, background and necessities of said minor children, in open Court asked
each of the parties and their respective attorneys if they had
objection to such investigation being conducted by the _____
County Welfare Department for the information of the Court, waiving
all technical objections they may have to such a report, such as
hearsay, and agreeing that the Court may consider such report for
whatever purpose he may deem proper, and each of the parties and
their respective attorneys consented to such investigation.

     It is therefore, ORDERED, ADJUDGED and DECREED, that an inves-
tigation be made by the _____ County Welfare Department into
the background, environment and necessities of the aforementioned
children, and to submit a written report to this Court not later
than _____, 19___.

                              _____
                              JUDGE PRESIDING

(Approved as to form and substance by attorneys and parties.)

No._____

IN THE INTEREST OF   )   IN THE DISTRICT COURT OF
)
_____   )   _____ COUNTY
)
A CHILD   )   _____ JUDICIAL DISTRICT

MOTION FOR ENFORCEMENT
OF A PRIOR ORDER

TO THE HONORABLE JUDGE OF SAID COURT:

COMES NOW, _____, Court-appointed Guardian ad
Litem for the minor child, _____, and moves and files
this Motion for Enforcement of a Prior Order of this Court, and in
support thereof would respectfully show unto the Court the following:

I

On or about the _____ day of _____, 19___, the Court
entered the following Order, a copy of which is attached thereto as
"Exhibit A," and incorporated herein for all purposes. Pursuant to
said Order, the Respondent, _____, was ruled to
deposit as security for costs the amount of _____
Hundred ($_____.00) Dollars within ____ days from the entry of
said Order.

II

Whereas, ____ days have passed since the date of said order,
and the Respondent has failed to file the deposit as security for
costs, and the Guardian ad Litem respectfully requests the Court to
cause a hearing to be held for the purposes of ascertaining why the
Respondent has failed and willfully disobeyed the Order of this
Court, and to show cause why such further and additional relief to
which the minor child may be entitled should not be granted forthwith.

III

Whereas, the Guardian ad Litem for the minor child has found it
necessary to seek this additional affirmative relief, said ad Litem
herein respectfully requests and moves that the Respondent be
required to pay reasonable attorney's fees for services rendered
herewith.

WHEREFORE, PREMISES CONSIDERED, the Guardian ad Litem for the
minor respectfully requests that this Court set a show cause hearing and that the Respondent be notified by service of certified
mail, return receipt requested, to show cause why the security
deposit as ordered on _____, 19___, should not be posted,
and why such other and further relief should not be granted by this

court and why reasonable attorney's fees should not be awarded, and for such other and further relief to which the Guardian ad Litem and the minor child may be entitled.

```
                              _____
                              Guardian ad Litem
                              Address:_____
                              Phone:_____
                              Bar Card Number:_____
```

STATE OF _____)
)
)
COUNTY OF _____)

    BEFORE ME, the undersigned authority, on this day personally appeared _____, who being by me first duly sworn, upon his oath states that (s)he is the Guardian ad Litem in the above and foregoing Motion, and that the facts and statements contained therein are true and correct.

```
                              _____
                              (Guardian ad Litem's signature)
```

IN THE DISTRICT COURT, JUVENILE DIVISION, WITHIN AND FOR

THE COUNTY OF _____ AND STATE OF _____

Juvenile No. _____; Div._____

THE PEOPLE OF THE STATE OF _____)
IN THE INTEREST OF:)
)
_____)
                  Child   )
)
ALLEGED TO BE   )   PRE-TRIAL
)   WITNESS & EXHIBIT LIST
_____)
              Petitioner   )
)
AND CONCERNING:)
)
_____)
              Respondent(s)   )

COMES NOW Petitioner, above-named, by and through _____
_____, Attorneys for Petitioner and the _____
County Department of Social Services, and endorses the Witnesses
and submits the Exhibits listed herein:

WITNESS(es)

_____   _____
Name   Address

_____   _____
Name   Address

_____   _____
Name   Address

_____   _____
Name   Address

_____   _____
Name   Address

_____   _____
Name   Address

_____   _____
Name   Address

EXHIBITS:

_____   _____

_____   _____

_____   _____

_____   _____

_____   _____

By:_____
Attorneys for the _____ County
Department of Social Services
Address:_____
Phone:_____

IN THE JUVENILE COURT IN AND FOR THE

_____ COUNTY OF _____

STATE OF _____

Action No._____

THE PEOPLE OF THE STATE OF _____   )
IN THE INTEREST OF:)
)
)
_____   )
                        Child(ren)   )   MOTION AND ORDER FOR
)   RELEASE OF INFORMATION
UPON THE PETITION OF:)
)
)
_____   )
                     Petitioner(s)   )
)
AND CONCERNING:)
)
)
_____   )
                    Respondent(s)   )

     COMES NOW the Guardian ad Litem_____
_____ for the child(ren)_____
_____, and moves this Court to Order any
medical institution, physician, psychologist or other medical
practitioner to release any and all information concerning the
child(ren)_____ in the above
entitled case. In support of said Motion, the Guardian ad Litem
states and alleges as follows:

     1. That in order to properly prepare and represent the minor
child(ren) in the above entitled case, the information requested is
a necessity.

     2. That the minor child(ren) are incapable of giving said
permission for release of said information on their own.

WHEREFORE the Guardian ad Litem in the above-entitled case moves this Honorable Court for an Order releasing any and all information concerning the child(ren) in the above-entitled case from any medical institution, physician, psychologist, or other medical practitioner.

Dated this _____ day of _____, 19___.

Respectfully submitted,

Attorney - Guardian ad Litem
Address:_____
Phone:_____

MOTION AND ORDER FOR
INTERVENTION

COMES NOW, the Applicant for Intervention, by and through her attorney, and moves this Honorable Court to enter an order pursuant to (state rule of civil procedure) granting her leave to intervene as a Respondent in the above captioned action.

AS GROUNDS THEREFORE, the Applicant states as follows:

1. That the Applicant has a right to intervene under (state rule of civil procedure) in that the Applicant claims an interest in the subject matter of the above captioned action, namely the custody of the minor child, or in the alternative that the Applicant be permitted to intervene pursuant to (state rule of civil procedure).

2. That the Applicant's interest is not adequately represented by the existing parties, and she is presently situated in such a way that the disposition of the above cited action may impair her ability to protect her interest in the aforementioned minor child if she is not allowed to intervene as a party to this action.

3. That the Applicant's claim for legal custody of the minor child and the pending above cited action have common questions of law and fact.

4. That the rights of the original parties will not be unduly prejudiced or delayed by allowing the intervention of _____, as a party to the above captioned action.

WHEREFORE, the Applicant prays this Honorable Court for an order granting this Motion to Intervene by right as a Respondent pursuant to (state rule of civil procedure) or in the alternative be permitted to intervene as a Respondent pursuant to (state rule of civil procedure) and for such other relief which the Court may deem just and proper under these circumstances.

Respectfully submitted,

Applicant's address   Attorney for Applicant
                                    Address:_____
_____   Phone:_____

IN THE DISTRICT COURT WITHIN AND FOR

THE COUNTY OF _____ AND STATE OF _____

Juvenile No. _____; Div._____

THE STATE OF _____   )
IN THE INTEREST OF   )
)
)
_____   )
                Child   )
)
ALLEGED TO BE   )   MOTION AND ORDER
)   TO TRANSFER CUSTODY
)
_____   )
                Petitioner   )
)
AND CONCERNING:)
)
)
_____   )
            Respondent(s)   )

COMES NOW, Petitioner, above-named by and through _____
_____, Attorneys for the _____ County
Department of Social Services, and moves this Honorable Court for
an Order to be entered herein forthwith granting a Transfer of
Custody of said child(ren) from their present placement to
_____
and as grounds therefore:

                              By:_____
                              Attorneys for the _____
                              County Department of Social
                              Services
                              Address:_____
                              Phone:_____

IN THE DISTRICT COURT WITHIN AND FOR

THE COUNTY OF _____ AND STATE OF _____

Juvenile No. J-_____; Div._____

THE PEOPLE OF THE STATE OF _____) IN THE INTEREST OF:)) _____) Child))) ALLEGED TO BE)) _____) Petitioner))) AND CONCERNING:)) _____) Respondents)	MOTION AND ORDER FOR PSYCHOLOGICAL EVALUATION

COMES NOW the Petitioner herein, Caseworker for the _____
_____ County Department of Social Services, by and through _____
_____, their attorneys, and moves this Court for an Order
to be entered herein for a psychological evaluation to be made and
submitted in regard to the Respondent

By:_____
Attorneys for Petitioner and
_____ County Department
of Social Services
Address:_____
Phone:_____

O R D E R

THE COURT now being duly advised upon the foregoing Motion and upon review of the file in the within entitled matter;

IT IS HEREBY ORDERED that a Psychological Evaluation be made and submitted in the within entitled matter in regard to the Respondent

DONE AND SIGNED IN OPEN COURT this _____ day of _____, 19___ at _____

BY THE COURT:

_____
JUDGE or REFEREE

```
                    IN THE JUVENILE COURT
            IN AND FOR THE CITY AND COUNTY OF _____
                         STATE OF _____
                    Civil Action No. _____
```

THE PEOPLE OF THE STATE OF _____)
)
In The Interest of:)
_____)
                      A Child   )
)
Upon the Petition of:)   MOTION FOR HOME EVALUATION
)
_____)
                    Petitioner

And Concerning:)
)
_____)
                    Respondents   )

    COMES NOW, the minor child, by and through his/her court-appointed Guardian, _____, and moves this Honorable Court to grant a Motion for Home Evaluation of the home of _____ and as grounds therefore states:

    1. That _____ are asking for temporary custody of the minor child, and hearing for such is scheduled for _____.

    2. That _____ had custody of the minor child prior to the commencement of this action and that placement with _____, who are relatives of the minor, would be preferable to continued placement in foster care.

    3. That the _____ are suitable custodian(s) for the minor child and have previously indicated their ability to properly care for the minor child prior to the commencement of this action.

    4. That the best interest of the minor would be assisted by such an evaluation in order to determine whether the home of _____ _____ continues to be an appropriate placement for said minor.

    WHEREFORE, the Guardian prays this Honorable Court to grant the above requested relief, and for such other and further relief as the Court deems proper.

Respectfully submitted,

_____
Guardian ad Litem
Address:_____
Phone:_____

MOTION FOR RESPONDENT
TO PRODUCE CHILD

_____, Court-appointed Guardian ad Litem for
_____ and _____, children, respectfully moves
this Court to enter its Order requiring the Respondent, _____
to produce immediately prior to the hearing next scheduled in this
matter on _____, the child known as _____,
and as grounds therefore alleges:

1. The present physical condition of _____ is
relevant to this upcoming hearing as a reflection of the effect of
her home environment.

2. The Guardian ad Litem will introduce evidence that _____
_____ is an abused child and the degree of abuse she has
suffered is reflected in her present physical condition.

3. Whether or not _____ and _____
should be returned to their mother, the Respondent in this action,
and the same home environment which has been detrimental to _____
_____ is an issue to be determined in the forthcoming
hearing.

4. The child _____ is approximately (age)_____
and not a party to this action, living in (state)_____ and
as such is not amenable to subpoena or her voluntary appearance in
this Court.

5. The child _____ is in the possession, custody
and control of the Respondent _____.

6. Pursuant to (state rule of civil procedure) the Court may
order a party to produce any tangible thing which constitutes or
contains matters within the scope of discovery and which is in the
possession custody, and control of the party upon whom the bequest
is served.

7. The interest of justice demand the presence of _____
_____ prior to the hearing and at the hearing on _____
_____ at _____ p.m.

Respectfully submitted,

_____
Guardian ad Litem
Address:_____
Phone:_____

STIPULATION TO PRODUCE CHILD

IT IS HEREBY STIPULATED between the parties hereto, as subscribed below, that _____ and _____ will produce immediately prior to the hearing scheduled at _____ a.m., their child known as _____ in _____.

IT IS SPECIFICALLY AGREED AND STIPULATED between the parties that the production of this child in _____ is only for the limited and special purpose of the aforementioned hearing, and the child is not subject to the jurisdiction of the Court nor the ___ _____ County Department of Social Services nor any similar agencies with respect to any alleged abuse upon the child which may have occurred outside the State of _____.

FURTHER, the Department of Social Services agrees not to attempt to obtain custody of the child, _____, while the said child is in the State of _____, for the limited purpose of the aforementioned hearing.

_____
Attorney for_____

_____
Appointed Guardian ad Litem
Address:_____
Phone:_____

_____
Attorney for _____ County
Department of Social Services

IN THE DISTRICT COURT WITHIN AND FOR

THE COUNTY OF _____ AND STATE OF _____

Juvenile No. _____; Div._____

THE PEOPLE OF THE STATE OF _____)
IN THE INTEREST OF   )
)
)
_____)
                Child   )
)
ALLEGED TO BE   )   MOTION AND ORDER FOR
)   FINANCIAL SUPPORT
)
_____)
              Petitioner   )
)
AND CONCERNING:)
)
)
_____)
              Respondent(s)   )

      COMES NOW Petitioner above-named, by and through _____
_____, Attorneys for _____ County Department
of Social Services, and moves this Court to order _____
_____ to provide financial support for the above named
child(ren), and as grounds for such Motion states the following:

By:_____

Address:_____

Phone:_____

MOTION FOR TERMINATION OF THE
PARENT-CHILD LEGAL RELATIONSHIP

Comes now the Guardian ad Litem and moves the Court to enter an order for the termination of the parent-child legal relationship of _____ and her parent, _____, in accordance with Section _____ of (relevant state statute).

1. As grounds for termination of the parent-child legal relationship, it is alleged: (a) that an appropriate treatment plan approved by the Court has not been reasonably complied with by the parent or has not been successful; (b) that the parent is unfit, in part due to the parent's incapacity to provide a safe and permanent environment for her child; (c) that the conduct or condition of the parent is unlikely to change within a reasonable time, especially as reasonable time is measured by the needs of the child, _____ _____.

2. Inasmuch as respondent parent has previously moved for independent evaluation at Court expense, the Guardian ad Litem joins in the respondent's motion for independent expert testimony under Section _____ of (relevant state statute).

3. It is requested that hearing on this petition for the termination of the parent-child legal relationship be held on _____ _____, 19___, or as soon thereafter as practicable.

                         _____
                         Guardian ad Litem
                         Address:_____
                         Phone:_____

The Referee, having read the foregoing motion, examined the record, heard the testimony of witnesses and statement of counsel, and being fully apprised in the premises DOTH HEREBY RECOMMEND that motion be granted and termination of the parent-child legal relationship be ordered.

                         _____
                         Referee

WHEREUPON the Court being now fully advised in the premises, doth approve the recommendations of the Referee and DOTH ORDER, ADJUDGE AND DECREE that said recommendations be entered of record as an order of this Court.

Done in open Court this _____ day of _____, 19___.

                         BY THE COURT:

                         _____
                         JUDGE

IN THE DISTRICT COURT IN AND FOR THE
COUNTY OF _____   No. _____
STATE OF _____   Filing Stamp

In the Matter of the Petition of

_____and

_____ for
the relinquishment of a child.

_____

PETITION FOR RELINQUISHMENT

    Come_ now _____ your petitioner_ and state
the following information:

    That the child the petitioner_ desire_ to relinquish is a child
born of the petitioner_ herein:

    That the same, age, race and religion of the parties are as
follows:

	Father	Mother	Child
Name			
Age			
Race			
Religion			

    That the child was born on the _____ day of
_____ 19___ at _____.

    Relinquishment is desired because:

WHEREFORE petitioner_ pray_ that an Order of Relinquishment be entered herein, terminating all of petitioner(s) rights in said child.

_____ and _____
being first duly sworn, upon oath, depose_ and say_ that _h_ ha_ read the foregoing petition, know_ the contents thereof and that the allegations contained herein are true.

_____

_____

Subscribed and sworn to before me this _____ day of _____,
19__.
Witness my hand and official seal.

My Commission expires_____

_____
Notary Public

(Mother's)
INTERROGATORIES

IN THE MATTER OF THE PETITION OF   Juvenile No. J-_____
                                          Division No. _____

_____

_____

RE RELINQUISHMENT OF A CHILD

What is your name?_____. Are you
over twenty-one years of age?_____. What are the race and
creed of the child who is the subject of relinquishment in this
action?_____. Are you
the mother of _____ born on _____ at
_____, this being the child
who is the subject of relinquishment named in this action?_____.
What is the name of the father of this child?_____
(if unknown, please explain circumstances of contact:_____
_____).
What is the age of the father of this child?_____. Were you ever
married to the father of this child at the time that the child was
conceived?_____. Were you married to a man other than the father
of this child at the time that the child was born?_____. If you
kept the child, the natural father of the child would be obligated
to support the child and if he failed to do so, you could sue him
for support money, do you know that?_____. Knowing that, do you
still feel that it is best to place the child for adoption?_____.
Do you know that you will never be able to change your mind about
this matter after the final Order of Relinquishment is entered?____
_____. Do you understand that you will never know in what home the
child has been placed?_____. Do you relinquish all of your legal
rights to the child and all of your obligations to the child in the
best interest of the child?_____. What are some of the reasons
for your thinking that this relinquishment is in the best interest
of the child?_____
_____.
If you want to talk to a lawyer you may do so; without cost to you
the Court will appoint a lawyer for you. Do you feel you need a
further explanation of your legal rights?_____. Have you been
thoroughly counseled by a Social Worker in this matter?_____.
What was his/her name?_____. Was any pres-
sure placed upon you by the Social Worker or by anyone else to
force you to arrive at the decision to relinquish your child?____.
Are you making this decision of your own free will?_____. Do you
wish more time in which to consider this matter further?_____.

_____
SIGNATURE OF MOTHER-PETITIONER

At the end of the hearing, when the Court has made a decision, you have a right to request a rehearing or new trial, but your request must be made in writing, within ten (10) days of the decision, unless the Court grants a longer time. If your request for rehearing is denied, you then have the right to appeal the Court's decision to the Colorado Court of Appeals.

STATE OF _____)
COUNTY OF _____) ss

_____, being first duly sworn, upon oath, deposes and says: That she has read the foregoing questions and that the answers written in her own handwriting are true of her own knowledge, except for those of which she has no knowledge, and as to them she believes them to be true.

SIGNATURE OF MOTHER-PETITIONER

Subscribed and sworn to before me this _____ day of _____, 19___, by the above named Mother-Petitioner.

My Commission Expires:_____.

NOTARY PUBLIC

(Repeat form for father)

GUARDIAN AD LITEM REPORT

Re:

This report is being submitted pursuant to Court order of _____ _____. The minor child has been seen by me on two occasions since the Dispositional hearing of _____. The purpose of these meetings was to observe the minor child, and look for factors that would indicate her adjustment since the dispositional hearing, specifically as those factors relate to assessment of her relationship with her prospective custodians, Mr. and Mrs. _____ and Ms. _____.

It appears that the minor child has maintained a warm relationship with at least Mrs. _____. Her relationship with Mr. _____ is in question in my mind as a result of certain statements made by the minor at my last meeting with her, and by virtue of certain developments in the _____ household since the dispositional hearing. The relationship between the minor and Ms. _____, seems to have returned more or less to its state prior to the termination of that relationship by the _____ after the death of the minor's mother.

The minor has been seen by a Psychologist, Dr. _____, who is recognized as an expert on parent-loss, on four occasions. The first two occasions for the purpose of evaluation pursuant to Court order upon the request of the Guardian, and the last two occasions for the purpose of beginning therapy. I have maintained a great deal of contact with Dr. _____ and I have had a lengthy discussion with him concerning the treatment needs of the minor child. Based on my discussion with Dr. _____, and I might point out that he expresses the same opinion regarding the minor's treatment, it is felt that offering treatment of the minor child cannot really commence until a more permanent decision is made regarding the minor's custodian(s). I am informed by the doctor that the minor's uncertainty as to her future has interfered with the limited therapy that has been done and that this uncertainty will prevent her from dealing with the more substantial issues she has to address, surrounding the death of her mother. Further, my discussion with Dr. _____ has indicated a need to reevaluate the relationship between the minor child and ___ _____ as it relates to the minor's development. Dr. _____ _____ will be available to testify at the Review hearing, and I will develop these areas with him on the witness stand.

The Guardian is extremely concerned about certain developments in the _____ household since the dispositional hearing. The _____ were separated for a time period, and during that period there was indicated an apparent unwillingness on the part of Mr. _____ to be involved with the minor's treatment. Further, this separation indicated an instability in the relationship between the _____ that contradicts the apparent closeness and warmth that was exhibited to the Court at the dispositional hearing. This separation further supports the feeling that the _____ have certain problems of their own that they have not dealt with, primarily around a psychological concept called the defense of denial. As a result of this development, I am concerned as to whether the personal problems of the ___ _____ are to such a degree that the minor's continued placement with them might jeopardize successful treatment and therapy for the minor. As of this writing, I do not believe that the _____ are involved in any type of individual therapy to deal with their own problems, and I doubt their ability to assist the minor in her therapy until this is done. These developments were also discussed with Dr. _____ and based on further consultation with Dr. _____, I fear the possible results the apparent instability of the _____ family will have on the minor's development and therapy.

With regard to Ms. _____, certain complaints have been made by the _____ that Ms. _____ is showering the minor with gifts and has a tendency to be over-indulgent regarding the desires of the minor child. This too was discussed with Dr. _____ and this would also have a negative effect upon the minor's treatment. This is an area of concern that would have to be addressed dealt with.

My conclusions, based on my conversation with the minor child, my observation of the minor child, my conversations with Dr. _____ _____, and the developments which have occurred since the dispositional hearing are as follows:

1.   The best interest of the minor child would be better served by awarding custody of the minor child to Ms. _____

2.   The instability of the _____ household has the potential of destroying effective therapy of the minor and posing more problems for the minor to deal with.

3.   The _____ must deal with some substantial personal problems before they can be really helpful to the minor's treatment.

4.   Visitation by the _____ with the minor child should be determined by the treating individuals in accordance with the treatment needs of the minor child as determined by Dr. _____ _____ and the treatment team.

5.   The award of custody should be a permanent one so that the minor child will know that she will be in one place.

Respectfully submitted,

_____

Guardian ad Litem
Address:_____
Phone:_____

INDEX

257